2⁵⁰

B1

COUP!

COUP!

Allende's Last Day

FLORENCIA VARAS and
JOSÉ MANUEL VERGARA

STEIN AND DAY/*Publishers*/New York

First published in 1975
Copyright © 1974 by Florencia Varas and José Manuel Vergara
Library of Congress Catalog Card No. 74-80900
All rights reserved
Designed by Ed Kaplin
Printed in the United States of America
Stein and Day /*Publishers*/ Scarborough House,
Briarcliff Manor, N. Y. 10510
ISBN 0-8128-1705-2

Contents

Contents

Preface

by FLORENCIA VARAS

On the afternoon of September 10, 1973, only a few hours before the coup would begin, I was in the Moneda Palace, attending a press conference given by Hortensia Allende, wife of the president, on her impressions of Mexico.

The press conference lasted for almost an hour. Without being able to define it, I felt a strange atmosphere of uncertainty. Every few minutes, a journalist would glance at the clock, obviously unable to keep track of what Mrs. Allende was saying.

I had been told by a press adviser that the following day President Allende would make a nationwide speech proposing a plebiscite on whether he should continue in office. A plebiscite would also give the troubled country at least sixty days of peace in which a political solution to the general economic paralysis might be arrived at.

On the morning of the eleventh, a Tuesday, I awoke to the sound of planes flying low over the city. My house, in the Alto section of Santiago, is only a few blocks from the air force academy. In the same section is the presidential residence.

I went immediately to the center of the city. Over the car radio I first heard the news of a military coup. It was 9:00 A.M. The streets were deserted, and except for the sound of a few explosions on the other side of the city, Santiago appeared already abandoned.

I took refuge in an apartment building two blocks from the Moneda. I watched the fight intensify. The ambulances went back and forth carrying the wounded. The noise from bullets and bombs grew louder. Each time I stuck my head out through the window, I was shot at by the police, who mistook me for a sniper.

From that vantage point I witnessed the isolation of Allende, increasing minute by minute, step by step. In a few short hours, the marches and slogans of his Popular Unity Coalition, that for three years had filled the streets of Santiago, were swept away forever.

"Allende, Allende, the people defend you!" the crowds had roared. On September 11, 1973, it was a sentence cut off in midair.

MAP OF
**CENTRAL
CHILE**

0   100   200
Scale of miles

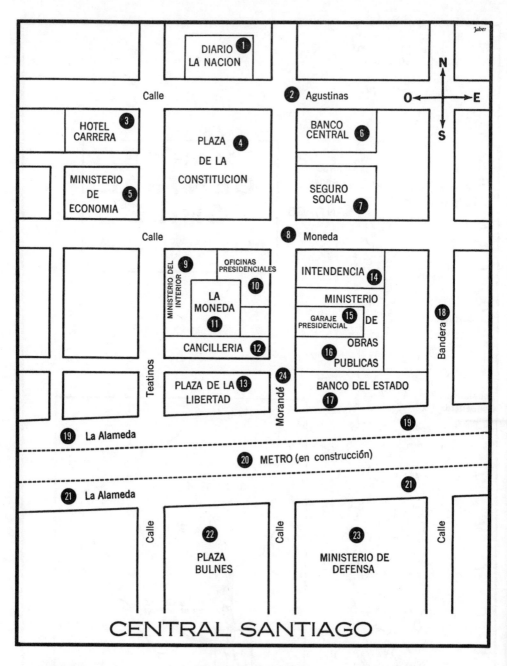

1 The Nation	**9** Ministry of the Interior	**17** State Bank
2 Agustin Avenue	**10** Presidential Offices	**18** Bandera Avenue
3 Carrera-Hilton Hotel	**11** The Moneda Palace	**19** The Mall
4 Constitution Plaza	**12** Ministry of Foreign Relations	**20** Subway construction site
5 Ministry of the Economy	**13** Liberty Plaza	**21** The Mall
6 Central Bank of Chile	**14** Offices of Administration	**22** Bulnes Plaza
7 Office of Social Security	**15** Presidential Garage	**23** Ministry of Defense
8 Moneda Avenue	**16** Ministry of Public Works	**24** Morande Avenue

EVENTS

At times I think I am dreaming. I cannot believe that this is real. After a while you realize it is real and that you either kill, or are killed.

Corporal Bernal, a carabinero

The First Steps

MIDNIGHT

A jeep and an army truck stopped in the poorly lit street. Four men and an officer, armed with machine guns and dressed in fatigues, jumped out of the jeep. At a signal the rest of the soldiers in the truck followed. Their movements were rapid and precise. They knew exactly what they had to do.

Peeking through the spy-hole in the door of the largest building on the street, a janitor saw the soldiers approach.

"Soldiers again," he thought. "The place is crawling with them these days!"

He cautiously kept the iron door closed.

Their footsteps drew closer. Behind him, on a rack inside the door, he had a rifle, but he doubted he would need it.

"Besides, it would be crazy. There's only one of me and lots of them, armed to the teeth." It didn't even occur to him to use the intercom to alert his friends in the rest of the building.

The soldiers had stopped outside the iron door. The officer's tone was brusque, his words like gunshots: "Open the door. This is a raid!"

Through his spy-hole the janitor could see two submachine guns pointed at him. Should he run? It would only get him shot. He took out the key and put it in the lock. The door was only open halfway when two soldiers slipped inside, pinned his arms to his sides, and shoved him before them into the courtyard of the broadcasting station on the outskirts of Santiago.

"How many people are here?" demanded the officer.

"Only six people from the night shift," stammered the janitor.

"Where are they?"

The janitor was pushed in the direction of his nod. "There are no weapons here," mumbled the janitor. It was lucky no one thought to look behind the door! There was not just his rifle!

"Shut up! We'll look ourselves!" replied the officer.

Once inside the building the soldiers spread out, searching. In the few minutes they had gathered all the night personnel in the entrance hall, with their hands above their heads, hemmed in by submachine guns. The men were searched for weapons, then allowed to sit in silence, guarded by four soldiers.

The broadcasting station was then systematically searched.

"There are no arms here," insisted another member of the night shift, but everyone knew he was lying. The Popular Unity Party had supplied all the radio stations with machine guns and hand grenades, in case of an attack by antigovernment forces.

In the lobby the sounds of the search were clearly audible.

"May I smoke?" asked one of the night shift. A gun barrel shoved in his face gave him his answer.

After an hour of fruitless search the soldiers returned to the hall. The men huddled in the circle of machine guns were exuberant. "Now do you believe I was telling you the truth?" said the janitor. "We have never had arms here, not even a knife. Why should we keep arms here?"

The officer in charge made no reply. He saluted the janitor, and he and the soldiers left the building.

The night personnel remained silent until the noise of the trucks faded, then burst into loud laughter. What they failed to realize was that those "soldiers" had achieved their objective: to break up the radio transmitter. In similar raids all over the country the broadcasting system was being dismantled.

In the Moneda Palace, the seat and symbol of Chilean democracy, the windows of the Presidential Office of Broadcasting, in the south wing of the palace, were still lit. The chief of broadcasting, René Largo Farias, exhausted after a fourteen-hour day, was annotating in the office's log book:

0005 hours:

I call the supervisor of Aconcagua about an apparent troop movement in that province. He agreed, "There is something going on." He will call back later with more details.

0010 hours:

I call the supervisor of Curicó about an apparent clash between peasants and soldiers. "That was at daybreak Saturday, comrade," he tells me. "There was a very serious confrontation between laborers and the army, but no casualties. Right now everything is under control, the incident is over, all is quiet in the province."

0018 hours:

I call the supervisor of Santiago to find out if he has any information regarding rumors of troop movements in the city. He said he would ask the rural police.

0025 hours:

The supervisor of Aconcagua called to confirm that unusual troop movements have been detected. The regiments "Guardia Vieja" of Los Andes and "Aconcagua" of San Felipe have been mobilized and were marching toward Santiago.

EVENTS

0028 hours:

I call Tomas Moro, the president's private residence, and am answered by Raul, a member of the presidential bodyguard, "the Personal Friends of the President" or GAP. I express my concern at the troop movements occurring across the country. He promises to convey my feelings to Comrade President, who at that moment is at a meeting with the minister of the interior and the minister of foreign relations.

0032 hours:

I try, for the third time tonight, to get in touch with the supervisor of Valparaíso, but I can't reach him. I can only ascertain that the fleet has embarked for its annual joint operations with the American navy.

0040 hours:

Report from the Prefecture General of the Carabineros: "Nothing unusual in the highways."

0110 hours:

Raul calls me from Dr. Allende's residence. He doesn't think we need to keep personnel to guard the Moneda. I send home the cameramen, the photographer, and the technicians of the radio department. The only people who stay behind are the journalist Pepe Echeverria, the radio-monitor Alex Sarmient, a chauffeur, and Sergio Jaque. There *must* be something wrong. We will stay behind in the office until things clear up.

0130 hours:

Because of the late hour only a few radio stations remain on the air. One is the National Radio Society of Agriculture, which keeps up a continuous attack on the government and the members of the Popular Unity Coalition. Alex transcribes a few paragraphs to send them first thing in the morning to the ministers and the president's private secretary.

0152 hours:

Comrade Sergio Jaque receives a call informing him that the regiment "Buin" of Santiago has had some shooting. Sergio makes various calls and confirms that "something funny is going on." Apparently the soldiers have been shooting at a vehicle that managed to escape.

0200 hours:

I call Carlos Jorquera, presidential press secretary, and I confide to him my fears that something strange is going on.

0210 hours:

I again call the Prefecture General of the Carabineros and the General Bureau of Investigations. Nothing unusual, they tell me, everything quiet with the exception of a few firecrackers which caused no damage.

0230 hours:

I talk with Alfredo Joignant, general director of investigations, who calms me down. Don't worry, man. These troops are loyal and will defend the legally constituted power against any disorders that may occur tomorrow. (At eleven o'clock the following morning a demonstration was planned by the Youth of the National Party in support of the truck drivers' strike.)

0235 hours:

We leave the palace.

On the way to his home, René Largo noticed an alarming bustle of cars and uniformed personnel around the gray building of the Ministry of Defense.

"I don't think we'll be able to celebrate the national holiday," he told his compãnera, Maria Cristina.

At the presidential residence, Tomas Moro, in the plush

residential quarter of Santiago called the Alto, the sixty-five members of the GAP were put on emergency alert. They paraded back and forth in the large gardens of the mansion, submachine guns cocked.

The majority of the guards were concentrated around the president's study, whose windows, overlooking the gardens, were still lit.

Inside, Salvador Allende, his minister of the interior, Carlos Briones, and his minister of defense, Orlando Letelier, were trying to decipher the most recently received information about troop movements in San Felipe and Los Andes, as well as the unexpected quartering of the troops in the Santiago Garrison, which his minister of defense knew nothing about.

Allende, nevertheless, seemed much more worried about the speech he would have to deliver at midday tomorrow, in which he would announce to the country his intention to call a plebiscite on his continuation in office.

At the moment, this political act seemed very much more important. He had become accustomed to unexplained troop movements during these last few months in government.

Late in the afternoon of the tenth, a Monday, while leaving his office in the Moneda Palace he had told newsmen: "I am absolutely convinced that we'll be able to survive these difficult hours."

Nevertheless, the minister of defense, in the early hours of the eleventh, decided to call General Herman Brady, chief of the Santiago Garrison, and ask him about these rumors about troop movements.

"What about San Felipe?"

"Nothing is happening in San Felipe."

"In Los Andes?"

"Nothing is happening in Los Andes, and even less is happening in Santiago. Everything is calm. There is nothing to worry about."

Reassured, Dr. Allende and his two ministers went back to drafting the speech for the next day. Allende's last day, the eleventh day of September 1973, had begun.

"The Fleet Has Returned"

DAWN

The cruisers, destroyers, submarines, and auxiliary vessels of the fleet were on the high seas. They had set sail from Valparaíso at 4:00 P.M. the day before, the tenth, to take part in joint maneuvers with units of the U.S. Marines.

Certain senior officers of the navy, led by Vice-Admiral Carvajal, at first refused to set sail. They wanted the government to accept the resignation of the commander in chief of the navy, Admiral Raul Montero, whom they considered Allende's man, and to have appointed in his place Vice-Admiral José Toribio Merino.

Several days earlier the president had refused to accept Montero's offered resignation, "until such time as, in the exercising of my legal and constitutional rights I reach a decision in this regard which in my estimation is the most appropriate and consistent with the interests of the country."

This decision had brought about a meeting in Valparaíso on September 9 of all the commanders and chiefs of naval units, presided over by Vice-Admiral Merino. Their deliberations were not made public.

The departure of the fleet was interpreted favorably by Salvador Allende, as a sign that, at least for the time being, the navy had agreed to continue under the leadership of Admiral Montero.

The sailors were as disquieted as their commanding officers. A group of their comrades in arms were being detained in Talcahuano and Valparaíso and were accused of subversion and extremism. There were rumors that they had been savagely tortured.

Only ten days before they had heard senator and secretary-general of the Socialist Party, Carlos Altamirano, say in a national address:

> The truth is that there has been a reunion among some of these navy people. I attended a meeting at which I was invited to listen to the complaints of the petty officers and some sailors about subversive acts perpetrated presumably by officers of that naval institution. I attended every time I was invited, in order to denounce some act or other against the legitimate and constitutional government of Salvador Allende.

Who really were the loyalists in the Chilean navy? Who were the conspirators? The answer was known at 0530 hours on the high seas, seventy-odd miles from Valparaíso.

All the crews of the fleet were told they were returning to Chile to support the overthrow of the legally elected government of Salvador Allende Gossens.

According to the naval high command this declaration was hailed with unanimous enthusiasm by both the officers and the sailors.

At dawn the cruisers, the destroyers, and the submarines were already at their battle places along the coast of Quintero, San Antonio, Viña del Mar, and Valparaíso. In Iquique, in Arica, in Antofagasta, Talcahuano, and Corral (the main ports of the country), the scenario was repeated. They had orders not to shoot.

The navy's involvement in the coup was to be limited to landing operations, if needed, by sailors and marines in support of the land forces. Otherwise, it was to stay offshore to present an eloquent testimony to their agreement with the events unfolding throughout the country.

With the first rays of the sun, thousands of still sleepy eyes peeping out from bedroom windows from one side to the other of Valparaíso Bay opened wide in astonishment—in terror or in delight.

"The fleet has returned!"

Among the early birds who were already aware of that fact were members of the armed forces and carabineros. At that precise moment, they were invading the city of Valparaíso, controlling all its strategic points, and neutralizing the probable areas of resistance.

Helicopters flew low over Valparaíso. The heads of thousands more inhabitants appeared at their windows. At first they were bad-tempered at being awakened. Then they ran to the radio to find out what was happening, but the radio was silent.

Some of the inhabitants of these coastal cities took the news very badly. They got dressed as fast as they could, grabbed whatever possessions they could carry, and left their houses. The great majority, no doubt, didn't get very far.

Valparaíso is a city quite easy to control. Most people lived in the hills. The guards, most of them dressed in navy uniforms, had only to barricade the road leading down to the port to capture the would-be escapees. A net had been flung over Chile.

"Halt! Show your documents!"

If you looked guilty, you were arrested. If not, you were told to go back home and stay there. Nobody wanted to argue with a gun pointing at his belly.

The Net Tightens

One colonel of the carabineros in Valparaíso didn't realize he was witnessing a general uprising of the armed forces.

Frantically, he called the national headquarters of the carabineros in Santiago on a special police line (all the others had been cut) and told the assistant chief of police, General Jorge Urrutia:

"Something weird is happening, general. There are navy people in the street, the radios are not working. A-1 communications are cut off, and the fleet, which sailed yesterday, has come back."

General Urrutia had also been unaware of plans for the coup. He immediately contacted the presidential residence, Tomas Moro, and repeated all he had just heard. At Tomas Moro the news came as a great shock.

The members of the GAP jumped out of their beds and grabbed their weapons. In the house's central hall Salvador Allende and Augusto Olivares, director of the national television channel and intimate friend of the president, were trying

25

to discover what was happening. Despite the apprehension felt by everyone, Allende remained calm and in control of the situation.

First, he asked Carlos Briones, who had left him only four hours before, to get to the Moneda Palace as soon as possible. Next, he spoke with the loyalist general director of the carabineros, José Maria Sepulveda, and ordered him to triple the guards at the Moneda Palace and bring up tank support.

Neither Allende nor Sepulveda knew the director had been substituted, a few hours before, by General Cesar Mendoza, a subordinate who was hostile to the Popular Unity Coalition.

The orders Allende had given Sepulveda would not be followed.

All three commanders in chief of the air, sea, and land forces could not be reached by Allende that morning.

The general of the army, Augusto Pinochet, and Air Force General Gustavo Leigh were not at their offices in the Ministry of Defense because they were already occupying their secret battle positions. The commander in chief of the navy, the loyalist Montero, was unavailable for quite different reasons.

During the night all his telephones had been disconnected and all his vehicles immobilized, isolating him in his house.

In addition, he too had been replaced: by Vice-Admiral José Toribio Merino.

Allende's call to the chief of the Santiago Garrison, General Herman Brady, did get through, but their conversation was not useful. Brady, who still knew nothing, promised to call back with more information.

Orlando Letelier, the minister of defense, was alerted at his home by another phone call from the presidential residence. When Letelier tried to call Valparaíso he discovered that all communications had been cut. He finally called his own ministry in Santiago and was answered by Vice-Admiral Patricio Carvajal.

"What's happening in Valparaíso?" he said as if he were talking of a remote planet.

"A few raids are being carried out in accordance with the Arms Control Law.

"You say you cannot communicate with Admiral Montero?" Carvajal continued. "He must have left his home to go to the ministry. . . . You are coming here as well? Yes sir, I'll wait for you."

As soon as Minister Letelier showed up at the ministry, a patrol detained him and quickly took him away to the Tacna Regiment. Vice-Admiral Carvajal was now indisputably in charge of the Defense Ministry.

There were some persons in the Ministry of Defense at that moment who remained in the dark. Commander Jaime Herrera, who had been on guard until the small hours of the morning, had noticed some suspicious activity during his shift, but he had been unable to discover anything and had gone to bed. He was wakened by a loud knock on his door. An officer in battle uniform told him: "Wake up Herrera, get up! Don't you see what is happening out there?"

Still half-asleep, Herrera tried to explain that he had been on guard and that he believed there had been several rather serious raids.

"What do you mean raids, you idiot!" exclaimed the officer. "Get up and look out the window."

In the parking lot in front of the ministry at least a hundred cars belonging to high officers of the armed forces had congregated: there must have been three hundred people already inside the building. "Good God," thought Herrera, "this must be more than a raid!"

The coup was not entirely unexpected. The official organ of the Communist Party, *El Siglo,* had printed a front page for September 11 whose upper half was taken up by a single phrase: "EVERYONE TO BATTLE POSITIONS."

The commando patrols of the armed forces had used the pretext of an arms raid under the Arms Control Law to enter radio stations all over the country and dismantle their transmission facilities. But several stations with mobile units managed to escape, among them, the Corporacion, Portales, and Magallanes stations. On the morning of September eleventh, they both rallied to the call by *El Siglo* and urged all the Popular Unity supporters to fight those seeking to overthrow the government.

René Largo Farias had been asleep for only four hours when a phone call from his sister Iris, wife of José Miguel Vargas, chief of press for National Television, woke him up. She told him that all communication lines with Valparaíso had been cut off and that the navy was engaged in an uprising.

While he was getting dressed the telephone rang again. A friend at the Moneda Palace told him the broadcasting studios of the State Technical University had been put out of operation. Largo Farias left immediately for the Moneda.

General Javier Palacios, director of army instructions, was in a military vehicle heading for the headquarters of the Second Tank Regiment in Santiago. He was due at seven o'clock.

General Palacios was worried. He had been ordered only the day before by the military junta directing the coup to occupy the Moneda Palace if Allende did not immediately surrender. To accomplish this mission the junta had put under his command the Second Tank Regiment, elements of which on June twenty-ninth of that year, under his own superior, Colonel Souper, had tried unsuccessfully to take the Moneda. (They had been defeated by their own comrades in arms, under the command of General Carlos Prats, a good friend of Allende.)

As a consequence of this abortive coup, many of the officers of the Second Tank Regiment had been court-martialed and confined to their barracks.

General Palacios was being asked, therefore, to confront these disgraced men and try to lead them on the same mission they had attempted a few months before. Would they obey him? What if some other officer defied him and pointed out that the Second Tank Regiment already had a commander ready to overthrow Allende and had no intention of following another?

What if someone else suggested the absurdity of being confined for an action which they were now asked to repeat? Hadn't they, in their own eyes, had good reason to attack the Moneda two months previously? Since now they were being asked to do it again, the army must agree with them. If so, why hadn't it backed them up then instead of turning against them?

General Palacios could not give any easy answer, but it was his task to assume command of the regiment and lead the column of tanks and armored vehicles once more against the Moneda.

All the Second Tank Regiment was assembled in the main yard of the regiment's barracks when General Palacios arrived. He identified himself and informed them that the commander in chief of the army, General Augusto Pinochet, and the commander of the Santiago Garrison, General Herman Brady, had given him command of the Second Tank Regiment and had ordered the regiment to accomplish the mission which they had failed to do two months before.

There was a silence. An officer came forward, saluted him, and asked, "Are you sure of what you are saying, general?"

All the regiment waited anxiously.

Without hesitation, General Palacios climbed up on a tank and shouted to the surprised regiment, "This is now under my command!"

As one man, the regiment fell in behind him.

At the same moment that the Second Tank Regiment, with Palacios at its lead, was heading toward the Moneda, Salvador Allende was preparing to go there also.

He had divided his bodyguard into three groups. The first consisted of twenty sharpshooters armed with automatic rifles. They would accompany him to the Moneda in four cars and a van loaded with thirty-caliber submachine guns and bazookas. The second group of twenty men would follow as soon as they had collected more arms and artillery. The third group of twenty-five would stay and defend the Tomas Moro residence.

President Allende was carrying an AK submachine gun, a gift from Fidel Castro which bore the inscription: "To my comrade in arms, Salvador."

The small presidential group actually started toward the Moneda at 0720 hours.

The joint command of Naval Zone Number One informed Vice-Admiral Carvajal at the Ministry of Defense in Santiago that Valparaíso had fallen and its provinces were totally under control. To everybody's great amazement, the overthrow had been done without firing a shot. A fight which had been expected to go on for at least three days had ended within one hour. In the ports of Valparaíso and Viña del Mar the inhabitants had sought refuge in their homes and given up any thought of resistance. All eyes were now turned to the capital city.

The Junta Speaks

At 7:30, Allende arrived at the Moneda Palace. Four bullet-proof Fiat 125s escorted the presidential car. Allende wore a gray sweater, tweed jacket, and rust-red pants and carried his submachine gun in one hand.

Once inside the building, he took complete charge.

The guard at the palace was made up of a select group of carabineros prepared to defend the government seat against the attack they knew must come in the next few hours. The GAP who had accompanied the president took up battle positions at the four corners of the palace on the second floor. A few stood guard at the door of the presidential office on the second floor with orders not to allow any member of the official armed forces to enter. It was a popular order: the GAP were not fond of the armed forces. They knew the top officers were anti-Allende and the armed forces as a whole intensely loyal to its commanders.

In turn, the armed forces thought the GAP an illegally armed group trained by foreigners (Cubans) which was breaking a century-old tradition; the custody of the Chilean president

31

had previously been the exclusive responsibility of the Chilean armed forces.

The president now met with everyone who was in the palace, which, to his surprise, did not include a single head of a Popular Unity party. He spoke calmly and decisively. He believed he could surmount the crisis with the help of a loyalist few. In any event, he was determined to remain at the Moneda Palace. The most important thing right now was to find out whom to trust in the armed forces.

José Maria Sepulveda, general director of the carabineros, had reinforced the guard outside the palace with three hundred of his men supported by tanks. But the general director had a nasty shock; his subordinates lacked their usual respect and hesitated at his orders. Something was going on.

August Olivares, on behalf of the president, was still unable to contact either army or navy chief. Brady, in charge of the Santiago Garrison and responsible for the defense of the city, had not called back with more information, as he had promised.

Olivares didn't know that Brady, like Montero, had been isolated. The telephone line connecting his office in the Ministry of Defense with the presidential office had been cut, at the order of Vice-Admiral Carvajal.

"With so many calls, General Brady was not able to be left alone to work in peace," the vice-admiral explained.

The remaining top officers of the armed forces were too busy taking care of their own tasks to attend to the calls from the Moneda. During those critical early hours of the coup, the president was not able to find out who was with him and who was against him.

Allende knew that if the armed forces were unified, they could overthrow him easily. All he could do in that case was make a desperate last stand. He did not want to involve the

poorly armed workers and peasants. To his cost, he had resisted
the suggestions from the extreme left of his coalition that the
workers and peasant be militarily prepared to support the government against the armed forces. Now it was too late. In fact,
factories had already been surrounded and street circulation
forbidden. In the initial confusion, many leaders of the people
had made good their escape.

In the buildings surrounding the Moneda housing the State
and Central Bank, the newspaper *The Nation,* the Ministry of
Public Works and Economy, and the Social Security Administration, there was an unusual amount of activity. Those em-
ployees belonging to the Popular Unity Coalition were taking
their battle stations on roofs or at strategic windows in response
to the Major Emergency Alert broadcast over Radio Magallanes. The majority of the three thousand loyalist workers in
these institutions were foreigners from Brazil, Uraguay, Bolivia,
Peru, and Argentina who had fled their own countries for political reasons and had been warmly received by the Popular
Unity. In Chile they worked as either students or technicians in
various universities or governmental agencies; they numbered
around 15,000. Seventy percent lived and worked in Santiago.

Many of these had some military training, particularly in
urban guerrilla warfare. Their future, should the Popular Unity
government fail, would be particularly uncertain. They would
probably be arrested and deported. Among all the groups as-
sembling in the early morning hours to defend the Moneda, this
"band of outsiders" had the most to lose.

At the Moneda, some important members of the Popular
Unity Coalition began to arrive. The tall, slender ex-minister of
defense, José Toha, reminiscent of a Castillian nobleman
sketched by Doré, announced to the newspapermen already

gathered at the entrance: "President Allende will remain in the Moneda. I have come to take my place with my comrade Allende. We will not hand over our mandate until November 3, 1976."

Carlos Briones, minister of the interior, arrived with Clodomiro Almeyda, minister of foreign relations, who had returned to Chile the day before from North Africa where he had been attending a conference of nonaligned countries.

Other arrivals were the minister of agriculture, Jaime Toha, brother of José Toha, and the minister of education, Enriques, Miriam Contreras, Allende's private secretary, and his two daughters, Beatriz and Isabel.

In a few minutes Enriques announced that he was going to work in his office as if this were just any normal day and left the building. (He would be in jail by "quitting" time.)

Inside the Moneda, no one knew if the carabineros were for or against the government. Generals Sepulveda, Urrutia, and Alvarez were repeatedly calling the prefect of police of Santiago, General Parada but were not able clearly to ascertain what was happening. Nor could anyone get a definite answer from other branches of the armed forces.

The ministers paced up and down the corridors. The members of the GAP inside the building kept a nervous eye on everyone there.

Outside, the palace guard, composed of carabineros, was swept by rumors. When was the attack to start? Would they be ordered to shoot their fellow policemen?

Orlando Letelier, minister of defense, had not yet arrived at the Moneda. Leaders of other parties in the Popular Unity were also absent. No one knew if they were organizing the working people's resistance or whether they had been arrested. No one suspected they were looking out solely for themselves.

Altamirana, for example, the head of the Socialist Party, had already gained refuge in the Cuban Embassy. Over the telephone, Allende harshly criticized General Parada for his indecision.

In the Office of Information and Radio Broadcasting, everybody was startled by the announcement which came over the radio:

> In view of the extremely serious social and moral crisis through which the country is passing, the inefficiency of the government in controlling chaos, and the steady increase of paramilitary groups trained by the parties of Popular Unity which would inevitably bring the people of Chile to a civil war, the armed forces and carabineros have decided:
>
> First, the president of the republic must immediately release all his powers to the armed forces and military police of Chile.
>
> Second, the armed forces and carabineros are united in their efforts to initiate the historical and responsible mission to fight for the freedom of the country and prevent it from falling under the Marxist yoke and to insure the restoration of order.
>
> Third, the workers of Chile can be assured that the economic and social achievements which have been reached to date will not undergo any fundamental change.
>
> Fourth, the press, radio stations, and television channels serving the Popular Unity must suspend their functions as news media forthwith. Otherwise they shall be punished.
>
> Fifth, the people of Santiago must remain in their homes in order to avoid becoming victims.

This proclamation had been signed by a junta made up of Augusto Pinochet Ugarte, commander in chief of the army, José

Toribio Merino, commander in chief of the navy, Gustavo Leigh, commander in chief of the air force, and Cesar Mendoza Duran, director general of the carabineros.

The voice of Allende spoke over the radio a few minutes later: "I shall not give up. I call on the workers to remain at their stations in the factory or plant. I am at this moment anticipating expressions of support from soldiers determined to defend their government. I renew my determination to continue to defend Chile. I intend to resist with what I have, even at the cost of my life. . . ."

Radio Corporacion and Radio Magallanes remained on the air, broadcasting two more statements by Allende to the people of Chile, but the battle of the radio was not evenly matched. The junta had control of many more stations: three out of five in Santiago and all of those based outside the capital city. They were combined to form a national network, and, starting off with the national anthem, they repeated over and over again both the proclamation of the junta and their first communique:

> Citizens are hereby warned that any act of sabotage of national activity such as businesses, factories, media, or transportation facilities shall incur the most drastic punishment possible at the place of occurrence and at the complete discretion of the local authorities.
>
> It is the duty of the citizens to keep intact the wealth of the country by reporting to the police immediately the names of all who try to paralyze production or engage in labor activities of any sort whatsoever.

The people of Santiago, like the people in Valparaíso, had been caught by surprise. They were still in their beds, or in the shower, or having breakfast, or on their way to work. Carabineros turned traffic away from the main thoroughfares leading to the center of the city, and enormous jams developed. Wherever they were, as soon as the junta made its first broadcast over the radio everyone was anxious to get home as quickly as possible.

On the other hand, few people in Santiago thought that the coup would be successful. They remembered the last attempt of June twenty-ninth, which had been immediately suppressed. The Second Tank Regiment rumbling through the center of Santiago had waited for the traffic lights to change before unleashing its attack on the Moneda.

In Tomas Moro the GAP kept close watch on movements in the surrounding streets and houses. They were already prepared to defend their position. The gardens and the rooms of the mansion had been divided into firing zones and each placed under a squad commander.

Inside the house Hortensia Bussi de Allende was listening to the radio and trying to follow events. The telephone rang. It was her husband.

"The navy has revolted, and Santiago is full of rioters. I don't know if we can hold out. Stay where you are, and try, Hortensia, try to keep calm."

"I hope it will turn out all right," she managed to say.

Meanwhile the commander in chief of the air forces, General Gustavo Leigh, had sent a terse message to the Ministry of Defense: "We shall bomb the Moneda at eleven."

Waiting for the Bombs

0830

Still suffering from an operation undergone only a few days before, Laura Allende de Pascal, a Socialist deputy and the president's sister, prepared to attend the Chamber of Deputies. She was as yet unaware of what was going on. On the way out the door, she was stopped by the telephone ringing. "Have you heard? No? Turn on the radio," a friend told her.

As if in a dream, she quickly learned the navy had staged an uprising in Valparaíso; the Moneda was surrounded by elements of the army; and her brother was trapped inside.

She could not bear to listen any longer and ran out to her car. Her one and only thought was to reach the Moneda as soon as possible, but her car would not start. Someone had cut a battery cable. She always left her car unlocked at night. The carabinero who stood guard at her home sat inside to escape the night cold. Where was he now?

In the end she was forced to ask a neighbor for help, and she lost a precious half an hour before she was on her way to the Moneda and her embattled brother.

The streets leading to the center of the city were still crammed with ordinary citizens who, unaware of the situation, just wanted to get to work. When she arrived at the Mapocho Station, Laura was held up by a carabinero with a submachine gun.

She tried getting out of her car and continuing on foot the rest of the way to the Moneda, but the policeman told her to get back into her car and turn around.

Laura had wanted to avoid identifying herself, but at this point she risked everything, hoping the carabinero might be intimidated enough to let her through.

"I am Laura Allende," she said.

Either the carabinero didn't hear her—there was a good deal of noise from the other cars—or he did not believe her. Whatever he thought, he did not allow her to continue toward the Moneda.

It was useless trying to get to her brother, thought Laura Allende, stuck inside her car, and now driving aimlessly. Even if this carabinero hadn't recognized her, someone would sooner or later.

Trying to keep a clear head, she remembered what her brother had told her to do in the event of a coup: she must immediately attempt to organize the other Popular Unity deputies.

By now it would be impossible to reach the central headquarters of the Socialist Party, which were in that part of the city already cordoned off by the armed forces. She headed instead for the Conchali quarter, where the party had a regional office. But when she arrived, twenty minutes later, she found no one she knew. Only a few confused members of the Batuco Socialist Party milled about. They had left their village because a helicopter full of soldiers had arrived that morning to "guard" Batuco's ammunition dump.

No knowing what else to do, Laura and the people from Batuco decided to go to the Cordillera regional office. It was the strongest and best organized base in all Chile. There, they could help prepare for the inevitable confrontation.

But when they reached the Cordillera office they found it as empty as the place they had left: only a few party members and one bewildered member of the Central Committee were to be found.

Laura kept searching for some party official who would know what to do. She visited the homes of five well-known Popular Unity leaders, but found no one.

In utter despair, she tried once more to reach the Moneda to join her brother.

It was on this trip that she heard over the radio the threat to bomb the Moneda. "Turn it off!" she sobbed to the comrade accompanying her.

In his home in Bulnes Street, a few blocks from the Moneda, Captain Grez, the navy's liaison to the president, was preparing to go to the palace. He was due for a stint as a reserve officer, which served as his vacation, but first had to clear up a few details.

At 0730 he heard a bulletin over the radio which upset all his plans. "Earlier this morning unusual carabinero movements were reported around the Moneda. Approximately two hundred carabineros and several tanks are now surrounding the palace."

Captain Grez immediately called his aide-de-camp at Tomas Moro, Commandant Badiola. A GAP informed him that neither Badiola nor the president was there.

Alarmed, Captain Grez called the Moneda, where a member of the palace guard said the president had arrived at 0740. Why Allende had arrived so early in the morning (he usually started his days at eleven), the man did not know.

At that moment Allende was broadcasting over the radio that in Valparaíso there was an "abnormal" situation and that a section of the navy was in revolt.

His week off forgotten, Captain Grez rushed out of his house heading toward the Moneda. When he arrived at 0835 he saw for himself the carabineros surrounding the building confronting the palace guards at the main entrance.

The captain, with his security escort and driver, was finally able to enter the building together with La Payita, Allende's private secretary, who arrived at the same moment with some other officials Grez did not recognize.

Inside the building, confusion reigned. Most of the security personnel carried submachine guns and had assumed battle positions in front of strategic doors and windows.

Grez found the president in his office surrounded by approximately thirty people: GAP, ministers of state, advisers, secretaries, and people from the Office of Information and Broadcasting (OIR).

Allende was trying to contact Radio Magallanes to broadcast his second proclamation. When he saw Captain Grez, he quipped, "Once again problems in your fleet, captain."

A few minutes later, Allende broadcast to the country over Radio Magallanes. The two other loyalist radio stations, Portales and Corporacion, had already been silenced. This was his last chance to talk to his fellow citizens before this station too would be put out of operation by the junta.

Captain Grez observed the effect on the president of the news members of the OIR brought him: the manifesto of the junta had just been published. The news "substantially altered his [previously] calm and confident manner." It was 9:10.

Ten minutes later, all the carabineros surrounding the Moneda began to withdraw.

Everyone inside the palace rushed to the windows.

The Moneda now stood defenseless. Allende had been counting on this force, not only in Santiago but across the country. They numbered some 25,000 men in all, but they must be obeying the orders of Director General Cesar Mendoza. The only allies left were the palace guard (made up of still loyal carabineros) and the handful of people around him.

At 9:25 Captain Grez's green telephone rang. Vice-Admiral Patricio Carvajal, chief of staff for the junta, was calling from the Ministry of Defense for the president.

According the Grez, Allende exchanged "ugly words" with the admiral when informed the junta had given him an ultimatum: if he would leave the palace immediately, he and his family would be allowed to leave the country alive.

Allende indignantly interrupted the vice-admiral.

"You have been conspiring for a long time, you vulture! And I won't forget it. You are mistaken if you think that I am going to allow this to go on."

Slamming down the phone, Allende reiterated to his followers his determination to remain at the Moneda, and then, calling his closest advisers around him, cleared the rest of the people out of the office.

Outside the conference room the three military liaisons to the president, Commander Badiola, Commandant Sanchez, and Captain Grez, agreed they should try to state their opinions privately to the president. They knew they were not trusted by the GAP or the president's closest advisers—Augusto Olivares and Private Secretary Osvaldo Puccio in particular. This mistrust was one reason the president had to ask twice that the office be cleared a few minutes later after he had granted their request to give them an audience.

This private conversation lasted no more than eight minutes. Each liaison officer related to the president his opinion of the situation and the futility of resisting the well-organized military forces with so few people.

Captain Grez spoke first.

"You must soften your posture if you wish to live. There is no possible resistance if the palace is attacked by the air force, the infantry, and tanks." Furthermore, the president must understand that he, Grez, was not willing to take up arms against the armed forces.

"I will not give myself up," Allende answered.

He would not relinquish his duties; he was not willing to negotiate with the commander in chief under these conditions; and he would remain in the Moneda and defend himself with his submachine gun from any aggressor.

"I shall fight to the bitter end, and the last bullet of the submachine gun I will shoot here . . . ," said Allende, and indicated his mouth with the index finger of his left hand.

"Gentlemen, return to your posts. That is all." Allende went to the next room, where his followers were waiting for him, informed them of his decision, and ordered that no one should impede the immediate departure of the liaison officers.

The officers waited a few minutes in case a GAP decided to attack on his own initiative. After ordering all navy personnel in the Moneda to withdraw, they left the palace by the door on 80 Morande Avenue.

The forces the junta had assigned to the Moneda, headed by General Javier Palacios, continued to maneuver. The carabinero forces with their tanks had been withdrawn. The Second Tank Regiment replaced them and was now stationed between Constitution Plaza and the *The Nation* offices. Its guns were trained on the Moneda.

The Infantry School Regiment of the Santiago Garrison was waiting in Augustin Avenue next to the Carrera-Hilton Hotel.

The Petty Officers School Regiment had spread out by the east wing of the palace, and the Tacna Regiment occupied the south sector, between the subway construction site and the Bulnes Plaza.

Still no shots had been fired.

The "zero" hour for the coup had been determined by the junta after cautious calculations. The chief concern had been the avoidance of "abnormality" in order to defuse popular reaction. If as few people as possible actually comprehended a coup was occurring, the operation could be carried out at a minimal "social cost" as had occurred in Valparaíso.

The traditional hour to overthrow a government is either at night or in the early morning, when the streets are empty and the factories and offices shut. But this hour would have required alerting the regiments of the Santiago Garrison the night before with the risk of a breakdown of secrecy.

Instead, a "normal hour" was chosen. At an earlier hour suspicion would have been aroused immediately. At a later hour, all the Popular Unity officials would have been at their desks and able to organize resistance.

Eight-thirty A.M. was the "zero" hour agreed upon, by which time the plan to dismantle all broadcasting facilities ("Operation Silence") must be completely executed.

By nine o'clock the junta chief of staff, Admiral Carvajal, had received the good news at his headquarters in the Ministry of Defense: The Communication and Telecommunication Service of the armed forces announced that, with the exception of the mobile unit of Radio Magallanes, the plan had been executed perfectly.

Those radio stations that had at first decided to remain on the air had now given in to pressure and joined the armed forces network. Others had been brought into line by nighttime commando operations under the aegis of the Arms Control Law, which authorized surprise raids for hidden arms.

In the case of radio stations that lacked independent power sources, the executors of Operation Silence had simply cut their lines.

Only the mobile unit of Radio Magallanes managed to continue broadcasting in support of the government.

The same pretext—an arms raid—had enabled the armed forces to place all public utilities such as electricity, water, gas, telephone, and oil under their "protection," without a shot being fired.

The College of Engineers, a projunta civil association headed by Eduardo Arriaga, was then placed in charge of keeping all these utilities in operation. Any attempts at retaking these installations were to be dealt with by the Ministry of Defense.

It had all gone like clockwork, and the junta could be well pleased with the progress of the coup.

All that remained was for Allende to relinquish his office, be placed aboard a plane with his family, and be sent abroad.

Resistance or Death?

Vice-Admiral Carvajal, in his capacity as chief of staff, met with Allende several times during the deliberations of the High Council of National Defense. (Made up of the president, the defense minister, the minister of the interior, and the joint chiefs of staff of the armed forces, it is in charge of national security.)

While the coup unfolded, the vice-admiral mulled over the meetings, which he always contemptuously thought of as "monologues by Allende answered by our silence. They were never really council meetings. Instead he would give a short pep talk telling us that the national security had been damaged by the CIA, and other reactionary elements from the interior of the country, who were behind the strikes. . . . In these meetings I could tell Allende was lying extraordinarily well, as were his ministers. Nothing could be believed. Allende certainly could lie diabolically well. I have a friend who is a very devout Catholic. One day he told me, 'I have found a description in the Bible describing Satan, it might as well be the description of Allende. I am firmly convinced he is a reincarnation of Satan.' You see, he had an incontestable ability to take people aside and lie to each individually and convinced them of anything."

Speaking to reporters shortly before nine thirty on the day of the coup, Carvajal was adamant: "The best thing for the country would be to send him abroad with his 'doctrine of lies.' "

At this point the three liaison officers to the president arrived at the Ministry of Defense and told Carvajal, "Allende won't surrender."

The officers added that Allende did wish to negotiate with the four members of the junta and requested they meet at the Moneda.

The prospect of negotiating with the president and his GAP was not very attractive to the junta. General Pinochet gave his staff liaison officer, General Ernesto Baeza, a peremptory reply: "The time for talks and conversations has already passed. Tell Allende we want him to surrender unconditionally."

It was a terrible moment for the president of Chile. His last hope had been negotiation. In a lifetime of politics he had always relied on negotiating his way out of anything. But the junta, holding all the cards, refused to budge.

When General Baeza gave the president General Pinochet's answer, Allende said, "Let them do what they want. They won't get me out of here alive. If they want they can kill me."

Up until this moment the battle had been strictly verbal. Numerous mediators searched desperately for a way to avoid bloodshed. The intercom lines between the Moneda Palace and the Ministry of Defense were overloaded. But the protagonists, President Allende and the junta, would not compromise. The other players realized that the conflict could only be resolved by force of arms.

"The time for words is over," the junta had declared. In the palace it was obvious to everyone. The time for bullets was approaching.

Snipers waited in battle positions in all the buildings that surrounded the Moneda. Inside the palace the GAP and the presidential guard lurked by doors and windows.

The most important variable in the developing crisis could be summarized in a question: will the workers fight? The "People's Power," based on those hundreds of thousands of workers in the industrial belt surrounding Santiago, had been invoked by the general secretary of the Socialist Party, Carlos Altamirano, two days before, in a speech at the Stadium in Santiago: "A reactionary coup is forestalled by a countercoup. It is not suppressed by conciliating with the mutinous. A coup cannot be fought with dialogues. A coup is crushed by the strength of the workers, by the strength of the people, by their district commanders, by the industrial cordons, by the peasants' councils."

His words were answered and echoed by the crowd of eighty-five thousand Socialist Party members, most of whom were workers: "No more deals! Now's the time to fight!" "Push ahead! No compromise!" "Build, build. Power to the People!"

The center of the city had now been given over to the contesting forces. Only soldiers, carabineros, or the Popular Unity snipers were visible. Most of the city had returned home or were confined to their places of work. The streets were empty. There was plenty of room for the bullets that were to come. Everyone waited for the battle to begin.

The second communiqué from the junta was broadcast over the radio: "The Moneda Palace must be evacuated before eleven. Otherwise, it shall be attacked by the national air force. The workers must remain at their places of work. If these orders are disobeyed, they shall be punished by the Chilean air and ground forces. Any sabotage attempt shall be drastically punished at the place of occurrence."

It was shortly followed by communiqué number three: "The population is warned not to be influenced by incitements to violence coming from national or foreign activists. Such activists must be made to understand that this country shall not accept any incitements to violence. They must relinquish any thoughts of extremism; otherwise, they will be immediately expelled from Chile or tried and punished by military tribunals."

Communiqué number four said: "It is most important that the youth of Chile have confidence in the country's destiny and in the armed forces, whose vigilance will insure their future and the future of our nation. The best way to cooperate with the new authorities is to obey all instructions. We call upon the fathers, in particular, to maintain a calm atmosphere in the family nucleus, to establish harmony throughout the nation. They must cooperate in the maintenance of order by insuring their children remain at home until order has been completely reestablished. There must be no public demonstrations including those claiming to support the new authorities."

In Valparaíso and Viña del Mar, where the coup was one and a half hours in advance, the junta-controlled radio stations announced that those who supported the new authorities should install Chilean flags in the windows of their homes.

By 10:00 A.M. both coastal cities were filled up with flags, and loud speakers from low-flying helicopters hailed the coup: "The hour for freedom has arrived for Chile. The armed forces have risen up against international Marxism. The hour of freedom has arrived for Chile."

Those who still had doubts as to who was in control of the

49

country only needed to look out to sea, where the navy warships stood ready for battle.

In Reraca the Armament School Regiment was busily convincing the inhabitants they should welcome the junta. The Coraceros Regiment was in charge of convincing Viña del Mar south. The Operations School Regiment devoted itself to convincing the skeptics in the Placeres Quarters. The school of military Engineers Regiment convinced those in the center of Valparaíso; the Maipo Regiment those on Ancha Beach. The School of Supplies Regiment convinced those of the central sector.

The Military Intelligence Service removed those who were extremely uncertain to the merchant ship *Maipo* and to a girls' high school which had been converted into jails for dissidents.

And if there was still some lingering doubt that the "hour of freedom" had come to Chile, the marines were in reserve.

Before the first bullet had been fired in Santiago, Valparaíso and Viña del Mar were displaying the flags of capitulation.

According to Naval Frigate Captain (R) Crispulo Escalona quoting Napoleon, "He who saves his country violates no law." At 10:00 in Santiago army troops under General Palacios clashed with the loyalist snipers attacking the Defense Ministry from adjacent buildings.

General Palacios wasted no time. He placed a tank in front of the Entel Tower, where the snipers' heaviest fire had come from, and "controlled" the situation. The rifle fire coming from the Moneda itself he answered with a cannon shell that shattered the door of the Ministry of Foreign Relations.

In the center of Santiago, the battle now broke out in earnest. Ex-president Jorge Alessandri peeped out from his riddled branch office in the Army Plaza and witnessed a furious duel between snipers stationed in the towers of the Cathedral and units of the army and the carabineros responding from the trees and monuments of the square.

A maid who worked for one of Alessandri's relatives in that quarter also peeped out the window to see what was going on—and was killed by a bullet in the head. The ex-president reported, "We told her until we were blue in the face not to look out the window."

The people of Santiago now heard the voice of Salvador Allende delivering his last speech over Radio Magallanes:

This will probably be the last opportunity I have to address you. The air force has already bombed the towers of Radio Portales and Radio Corporacion. But my words are not spoken in bitterness, rather, in disappointment.

Let there be a moral judgment on those who have betrayed the oath they took as Chilean soldiers and commanders in chief: Admiral Merino, who has appointed himself commander in chief of the navy, Mr. Mendoza, an abject general who only yesterday declared his loyalty to the government and who today has appointed himself general director of the carabineros.

In the face of these events all that remains for me to say to the workers is, "I shall not surrender." Placed in a crucial moment of our history, I will pay with my life for the loyalty of the people. And I tell you I am certain the seed which has been planted in the conscience of thousands and thousands of Chileans shall not be totally uprooted. They are strong, they are able to subdue us, but social processes cannot be detained by either crime or force. History is on our side, and it is made by the people.

Workers of my fatherland, I thank you for the loyalty you have always shown me, the confidence you have placed in a man who was a mere interpreter of your deep yearnings for justice, who pledged his word to defend the constitution and the law and who has kept it.

In these final hours before my voice is silenced, I want to make one point. It was the united reactionary forces of foreign capital and imperialism that created the climate for the army to break their tradition . . .

I wish to speak most of all to the modest women of our land, to the peasant women who believed in us, to the working women who wished to work more, to the mothers who knew of our concern for their children.

I address the professionals of our country, those who kept on working despite the sedition encouraged by the professional colleges, elitist institutions which would defend the advantages a capitalistic society grants them for its own ends.

I address the youths of Chile, those who sang, who gave their joy and fighting spirit to the struggle.

I address the men of Chile, the worker, the peasant, the intellectual, all of whom shall be persecuted. In our country, fascism has been present for some time—evidenced in the terrorist actions which blew up bridges, cut railway lines, destroyed pipelines, all done in the face of the silence of those who should have been responsible. They were compromised, and history shall judge them.

Radio Magallanes will surely soon be silenced, and the calm tone of my voice will no longer reach you. It does not matter. You shall continue to hear it. I shall always be with you, and you will remember me as a dignified man who was loyal to his country.

The people must defend themselves, but not sacrifice themselves. The people shall not let themselves be destroyed nor demolished, but they shall not let themselves be humiliated either.

Workers of my fatherland, I believe in Chile and in her destiny. Other men will survive this bitter and gray moment in which treason is trying to take the upper hand. Just remember, sooner than you think avenues shall again be opened down which free men shall march toward a better society.

Long live Chile! Long live the people! Long live the workers! These are my last words. I am convinced my sacrifice shall not be in vain. I am convinced that, at least, it shall serve as a moral judgment on felony, cowardice and treason that lay waste our land.

"They Shall Not Move Us"

The battle around the Moneda had intensified. The army was under fire constantly, particularly from snipers sheltered in the Ministry of Public Works.

Vice-Admiral Carvajal in the Ministry of Defense received another call from the palace, from the ex-minister and close friend of Allende, José Toha.

It was the politest of exchanges.

Toha: "Admiral, would you grant me ten minutes to convince the president to leave the palace before we are bombed?"

"With the greatest of pleasures, Mr. Toha."

"If I may ask another favor, will you stop firing so that we can continue our conversation undisturbed?"

"I would be more than willing, Mr. Toha; however, your snipers insist on bothering us, especially those from the Ministry of Public Works, and we are obliged to respond."

"Of course, of course, but who knows, maybe an order from you and—"

"Unfortunately your snipers are not willing to listen to an

order given by me, Mr. Toha. And time is running out. The air force has already been given its orders. The planes may arrive at any moment—"

"I have tried everything in my power to try to convince the president, but—"

"Well then, throw him out by force."

"Ah, but he is armed with a submachine gun. Why don't you try talking to him, admiral? Perhaps your arguments shall be more—convincing than mine."

"What? I, talk with Allende? You can't ever talk with that man. All he does is insult you."

"Well, then, I'll see what I can do," promised Toha, hanging up.

In the Moneda, René Largo Farias had gathered all the personnel of the Office of Information and Broadcasting and, nervously making a few jokes, urged them to leave the encircled building anyway they could.

The last one to leave was a lieutenant-major of the carabineros who had been assigned to the office.

"Sobbing, he hugged me," Farias reported, "trying to say something, but seemed choked by tears and by his helplessness in the face of treason."

When they had all left, Largo Farias dialed the president's extension and was answered by Allende himself. He asked for instructions, and the president answered, "Well, those who wish to fight with me can stay. Let them come up."

José Toha and the minister of the interior, Carlos Briones, had tried, but failed, to convince the president to surrender. Apparently Allende still believed that he and his few supporters could withstand the military forces surrounding the Moneda for a time. The junta would not dare use the tanks or heavy guns or bomb the palace, for fear of destroying the entire center of

Santiago, including the most important symbol of Chilean democracy, the presidential palace. The longer they held out, the greater the (public) pressure on the junta to negotiate, or so the president thought. Besides he didn't think much of the army's tanks.

Mario Arnello, a National Party deputy, later recounted that after the June 29 tank attack Allende had spoken sarcastically about the "little tanks" Colonel Souper had used to assault the Moneda, which could be held back with a few rifles.

Allende's remarks had so mortified General Pinochet (who was to head the junta) that, without breathing a word to anyone, he ordered a thorough overhaul and immediate repairs be made to some idle Sherman tanks. It was these tanks of higher tonnage and greater firing capacity than those Souper had used which surrounded the Moneda on the eleventh.

Allende didn't think much of the air force either. General Gustavo Leigh, commander in chief of the air forces, reported Allende telling him, "I'll buy you some planes, general, but good planes, not like those junk heaps you have now."

At this moment on the morning of the eleventh, General Leigh was getting his Hawker Hunters ready. On recalling those words of the president, he commented, "Now that quack will see what these little jalopies can do."

Allende was clinging to the idea of embarrassing the junta into compromise by the spectacle of forty or fifty men resisting an army of thousands; however, he soon had another unexpected blow. The new director general had ordered the palace guard to withdraw.

None of the carabineros waited to have the order repeated; they left the Moneda immediately to take refuge in the cellars of Constitution Plaza, where their comrades in arms welcomed them.

Opposite the entrance to the Moneda on Morande Avenue

stood the presidential garage. A group of carabineros, armed with submachine guns, had just captured the trucks carrying the arms from Tomas Moro. The twenty accompanying GAP members were also arrested.

The palace was now enveloped by a menacing silence.

All over Santiago, people looked up at the sky and counted each passing minute. A few broke out champagne to celebrate the inevitable.

Eleven was the deadline.

Only a half an hour remained before the bombing was scheduled to begin. It was a unique experience for a Chilean city. The people of Santiago waited, still incredulous, for an event they had previously only seen at the movies.

The armed forces had withdrawn from around the Moneda to make room for the bombs. The only people left in the area were some journalists crouched in strategic places and ready to capture on film the inconceivable: the destruction of this historical seat of government with the legally elected president and the majority of his ministers inside.

The Moneda was a national symbol. The building itself expressed certain "Chilean" characteristics. It was a subdued gray, of no great height. Its base was broad and strongly built. Its colonial patios were open to the sky. Above all, the Moneda was a hospitable building through which waves of both Chileans and foreigners had passed freely, as if along an avenue dedicated to democracy, for many generations and twenty-seven popularly elected presidencies.

Beatriz Allende, daughter of the president and one of the eleven women who had decided to remain in the palace, remembered that her father remained calm, even at this desperate moment. He listened to various reports; he gave orders and curt answers. He himself checked all the battle stations in the palace and corrected the firing positions of his comrades. He ordered that the safest places in the Moneda be designated as bomb shelters for those supporters who remained.

The eight physicians to the presidency were to keep the surgical pavilion ready to take care of the wounded. He appointed a comrade to organize the women and take them to a safe hiding place until he could convince them to leave the Moneda.

He ordered all personal documents which might subsequently compromise other revolutionaries to be burned. He sent three comrades out of the palace, two of them women, to organize a future resistance.

Beatriz had a short meeting alone with her father. The president reiterated his decision to remain fighting to the end. The outcome was already quite clear to him, but he would see to it that the fighting would be carried out in the best possible manner. The fight was going to be hard, and he was at a disadvantage; nevertheless, this was the only way he could behave as a revolutionary and as a constitutional president defending the authority conferred upon him by the people.

By refusing to surrender he would stand witness to the treason of the military forces and their fascist leaders. Finally, he expressed again his concern for the women comrades who remained in the palace, for his other daughter Isabel, for his wife, who was still at Tomas Moro, where fighting was going on.

In a way, Allende told his daughters, he felt relieved that this moment had arrived. Everything was clear now. He was freed from the uncomfortable situation of being president of a government dedicated to the people but which was forced to tolerate an armed forces who repressed the workers by raiding industries and harassing the laborers.

Beatriz thought her father's morale that morning was amazing and inspiring. There was no question in her mind that he was ready to fight.

The important thing now, her father told her, was the political direction of the future. A common objective for all the revolutionary forces must be established. The workers would need a united political direction. For that very reason he wished no futile sacrifices. Instead, the vigorous struggle for this united political direction must be begun that very day.

"Viva La Revolution!"

"Here they come! Here they come!" shouted two excited children, pointing toward the south. The planes were coming from Concepción, two hundred and fifty miles south of Santiago, a base that seemed safer than that of El Bosque or that of Cerrillos, which were too near the potentially volatile industrial belt surrounding Santiago.

They passed behind San Cristobal's hill, flew farther north, flew back, maneuvering. Santiago watched in awe and silence as the planes zeroed in on the Moneda.

At that moment Radio Magallanes went off the air. The last things René Largo Farias heard were the Radio Magallanes journalist Guillermo Ravest calling upon the people to defend themselves and then the first bars of the song "They shall not move us!" made famous by the defenders of Madrid against Franco's forces in the Spanish Civil War.

In the few minutes before eleven that remained, Largo Farias climbed the old stone staircase separating the Office of Information on the first floor from the presidential offices on the second floor. He entered the Toesca Salon, named in honor of the Moneda's Italian architect, a large rectangular room paneled in wood, and found the president.

Allende was wearing an olive green steel helmet and carrying his submachine gun. He was surrounded by the ministers and ex-ministers who had decided to remain with him: Minister of the Interior Carlos Briones, Minister of Agriculture Jaime Toha, Minister of Foreign Relations Clodomiro Almeyda, Undersecretary of the Interior Daniel Vergara, and the ex-Minister of Defense and of the Interior, José Toha.

Also in the room were Osvaldo Puccio, Allende's private secretary, and his son, a member of the Movement of the Revolutionary Left.

About forty people altogether were there, including Anibal Palma and Fernando Flores, the general governmental secretary; Augusto Olivares, José Vargas, the chief of press for National Television; Eduardo Paredes and Arsenio Poupin, of the National Bureau of Investigation; Jaime Barrios, manager of the Central Bank; and the entire staff of the Office of Information. Finally, there was the group of women, whom Largo Farias did not recognize, those members of the GAP not on guard, and a group of doctors.

The atmosphere was hectic. Some people kept checking their weapons; others whispered together or looked preoccupied. Suddenly, Allende's voice silenced the room.

"The women and the men who are not armed must leave. I *order* that the women comrades abandon the Moneda. I want them to leave. I am not going to surrender, but I don't want any sterile sacrifices. Revolutions are not made with cowards at their head. For this reason I shall remain here. Everyone must come to their own decisions. Those who would stay and fight must have weapons and know how to use them. The others must go."

The minister of the interior urged the president once more to try to negotiate with the junta.

Allende only replied, "I shall fight till the end. They will have to carry me out dead." Briones realized then that Allende must be on another wavelength. He no longer had any private conferences but preferred to remain surrounded by those supporters who wished to stick by him to the end.

Briones wondered if Allende at the end of his long political career was realizing a suppressed guerrilla vocation. Was he in these last moments consciously imitating his admired friends Fidel Castro and Che Guevara?

Carlos Briones believed everything was over: the government and its president were finished.

He hardly recognized in that man wearing a helmet and carrying a submachine gun the Allende he had known for twenty-five years: cordial, courteous, a great orator and exponent of political solutions. He had never guessed at this side of Allende which he could only describe as "irrational."

It made it impossible to speak to him, to find a meeting ground. Only a few hours before in Tomas Moro, Briones had conversed with the usual Allende who, although he realized the situation was desperate, did not believe his government was done for and that even his death would be so near.

At which moment of that dramatic morning did this rupture occur in the personality of the president who now appeared "in another plane," according to one of his oldest colleagues? Might the cordial and courteous Allende, the great orator and political exponent have given up the ghost when he found out his words accomplished nothing in the face of an inflexible and monolithic army prepared for battle?

The Bombing of the Moneda

1130

In the Ministry of Defense, General Baeza, the liaison between the junta and the ministry, counted the minutes anxiously.

When there were only fifteen minutes to the agreed hour for the bombing, there was a buzz from the intercom connecting the ministry to the Moneda. It was Allende.

"I ask for ten minutes to let the women go," he said, and added, "No man will leave."

General Baeza answered that the attack would begin at eleven, that there was still time for him to surrender and leave with his family in the plane that was waiting.

Allende again refused.

The general pleaded with him. "I beg of you to soften your attitude. Don't lead all those people to a disaster. The air forces will attack first, then the tanks, then the infantry. . . ."

Allende would not surrender.

Allende then talked to Vice-Admiral Carvajal. "Admiral, I

beg of you to let the six women who are here leave the palace. Among them is one of my daughters, who is pregnant. It is your duty as a human being to allow her to leave."

"I understand perfectly. We'll let them leave."

"I want a vehicle with an officer to give them protection."

"Fine, I will send a vehicle with an officer."

"I want you to give me your word of honor that you are not going to shoot them."

"How can they be shot?"

"There are some who might do it, some fascists."

"What fascists are you talking about?"

"I am not referring to you personally, admiral, but there are some people who may shoot."

The admiral later observed that between his first communication with Allende and this one there had been a considerable change in the president's tone: it was now much more subdued.

Ten or more unarmed people had gathered in a narrow cellar of the Moneda in anticipation of the bombing. Among them were Isabel and Beatriz Allende and René Largo Farias. Suddenly Allende appeared, flanked by his bodyguards, the faithful GAP.

"I have General Baeza's word that there will be a cease-fire of five minutes to allow the women to leave," he said.

"Papa you still believe in the word of a soldier!" Isabel Allende exclaimed.

"I still believe in it," Allende answered.

"They will take us as hostages," said Beatriz. "They will kill us."

"It would be better if they killed you then, rather than now. History would judge them not only as traitors, but also as murderers of women. But please leave, Isabel. You have a mother to take care of. You Taty [Beatriz] have children, you have your husband in the Cuban Embassy. You must be near him."

Both women continued to insist they wanted to stay. Finally Allende told them, "If you don't leave I shall be forced to go out in the street with you."

René Largo Farias realized that Isabel was near breakdown. She began to cry. She kissed her father and left the cellar. But Beatriz lingered a few more seconds. She stared fixedly at Allende, as if to memorize every feature. Finally she got up, embraced her father tightly, and followed Isabel.

The inhabitants of Santiago gaped at the sky, as they waited for the circling planes to disgorge. Accustomed to earthquakes, Santiago was bewildered by the idea of bombs.

In the Ministry of Defense there was frantic activity. The decision made in the last few minutes to postpone the bombing until 1130 had to be communicated to the Hawker Hunters. The planes were already in position and about to attack. Then the orders got through, and the surprised pilots were told to suspend the bombing.

At the Ministry of Defense there was a unanimous sigh of relief when the planes were seen to withdraw. In the Moneda a group of women and a larger group of men were leaving by the entrance on Morande Avenue.

Allende's two daughters led the party, crouched on all fours to avoid the cross fire between the snipers and soldiers. Beatriz Allende, whose pregnancy was in an advanced state, felt contractions. Nevertheless, she continued moving through the deserted streets, plastering herself against the walls. She and her sister managed to reach the lobby of a fashionable hotel close to the Moneda.

The appearance of two exhausted women aroused the manager's suspicion. He thought they must be running from the police, refused their money and, instead, ordered them to leave before getting him into trouble. Once again Isabel and Beatriz found themselves in the street. They would have to find another place of refuge.

During the half an hour of respite before the Hawker Hunters were scheduled to return, everyone in the cellar had left the Moneda except Largo Farias. He made the most of those last few moments by reconstructing and committing to any available scrap of paper what Allende had said to him in the Toesca hall. On the back he wrote a farewell message to his wife and seven-year-old child. He had no doubt that he would die.

At that moment Jorquera entered the cellar. He carried a bottle of whiskey in one hand and a glass in the other. Largo Farias and his wife used to hold folk music gatherings every week in their home, and Jorquera had often attended them.

"If I could find a folk dance group I would dance the 'cueca' . . . but there are no guitars, so let's drink the last drink of our life in the glass of our president."

And he poured the whiskey. But they were not alone in drinking Allende's health.

Miriam Contreras Bell de Ropert was known as "La Payita."

She was forty-six years old, of normal stature, and unusually attractive, with beautiful and expressive blue eyes and full lips. In 1950 she had married Enrique Ropert, an engineer with socialist ideas, and had established their home in a house on Guardia Vieja Street. Their next door neighbors at Number 398 were the Allende Bussi. The families became very close. The daughters of Salvador Allende had only to cross a door especially built through the adjoining garden wall in order to take advantage of the Ropert's swimming pool.

The Roperts had helped to finance Allende's presidential campaigns. After the last successful election, Payita had become

Allende's indispensable personal secretary. She had left her home on Guardia Vieja Street and moved to the house that Allende had bought her, near the Cordillera: El Canaveral.

Laura Allende, the president's sister, had thought that Payita was an extraordinary woman who lived only to take care of and to serve Salvador. A true "geisha" she had won not only Salvador's love, but also that of his daughters and sister. Besides her tasks as private secretary she was the "Mother Superior" of the GAP, the generally unpopular presidential bodyguard. She looked after their meals and gained the loyalty and the respect of that difficult group of "James Bonds." A considerable number of them lived in Tomas Moro, as well as in La Payita's own house. There they practiced guerrilla arts, and, Payita, mother superior of this peculiar order, was even taught how to handle arms.

At the Moneda she drafted the memos for Allende's speeches and kept the room next to his presidential office ready for his nap after lunch. She would draw the drapes, order silence, and then disappear.

Dominating both the entrance of El Canaveral and Payita's life was a large portrait of Allende with the following inscription: "To Payita, my best friend and great comrade with my best wishes for her and her family. With great affection, Salvador, Sept. 5, 1970." It was the crowning day of Allende's political career.

On this eleventh day of September, 1973, Payita hid in a cellar because she did not want to be separated from Salvador on this day of bitterness and defeat.

She emerged from her hiding place and smiled at Largo Farias and the "black" Jorquera. From the stairs they could hear Allende's voice calling: "Paya, Paya, where are you? Where have you got to?"

La Payita, with a finger to her lips, signaled to Largo and Jorquera not to give her presence away.

It was the last time Largo Farias heard Allende's voice. Soon afterward, Jorquera and La Payita went somewhere, and he was left alone in the cellar, in a silence he found terrifying. It stank of smoke from the burning of documents that might have compromised those who would organize the future clandestine struggle against the junta.

Finally, he staggered up the stairs and walked through the deserted Presidential Gallery and down to the Winter Patio. There, someone offered him a weapon which he refused. He didn't know how to handle a weapon. Never in his life had he treated anything with so much contempt. A familiar voice accosted him.

"What are you doing here, you idiot! Go home. You are going to be more useful outside than stuck in this mousetrap. Here they are going to blast everyone's head off. Please go away...." It was Augusto Olivares. Adding action to words, he pushed Farias toward the door on Morande Avenue and said goodbye, "You have to leave this place with you hands up...."

Time passed. Only a few minutes were left until the deadline. The women had all left, with the exception of Payita, who had emerged from her hiding place and now stuck close to Allende's side.

The president and those who decided to remain with him now descended to the cellar of the Winter Garden to wait for the bombing there. Carlos Briones, Clodomiro Almeyda, the two Tohas, and Anibal Palma arrived a few minutes after the main party, but they discovered there was no room. The cellar was already filled by Allende, La Payita, Daniel Vergara, Osvaldo Puccio, and members of the GAP.

The five men rushed over to the wing of the palace which housed the Ministry of Foreign Relations. They had heard there was another cellar there.

Breathlessly they crossed an open patio with bullets hissing overhead and walked through bullet riddled passages to finally arrive at the ministry. But the minister of foreign relations could not remember where the damn cellar was!

In the course of their frantic search they encountered a minor official from the ministry, Ernesto Espinoza, and a certain Mr. Silva, of the Office of Information, who had been unable to escape with the others.

Ernesto Espinoza was better informed than Briones and led the way to the cellar. To reach it they had to knock down a few doors. In the end, the cellar turned out to be only the boiler room of the ministry, but it still seemed a safe place, and they all squeezed in to wait for the bombing.

René Largo suddenly found himself in the middle of Morande Avenue, his arms raised. He began to advance in an eerily empty world. He walked slowly up to the Offices of Administration with his hands still held above his head. He glanced to the right, and then to the left: nobody. There was not a soldier, not a tank, nothing, only a few reporters taking cover near the Administration building. He turned right into Moneda Avenue and continued to advance until he reached Bandera Street without even knowing where he was going. No one called out to him, no one rose up to detain him. Slowly he retraced his steps through the seven streets that separated him from his home in Alonso Ovalle.

While he embraced his sobbing wife and child, they shuddered from the sound of the first rocket that exploded on the Moneda.

The Hawker Hunters had again taken off from Concepción and made their first flyover of the Moneda at 1152. During each flyover the two planes left four rockets embedded in the north wing of the palace, that now spewed a thick column of smoke. A minute later the operation was repeated. During twenty minutes the Hawker Hunters passed over eight times. By 1213 the north wing of the Moneda was a mountain of hot, twisted iron and burning wood; but not a single adjacent building had been affected, except by the noise, the trembling of the earth, and the panic.

In fact, only that wing of the palace in which the presidential offices were located was hit. What had seemed impossible only a few hours before had become a reality.

The Hawker Hunters returned to their base to reload. Their orders were to duplicate the attack on the Tomas Moro residence, where the GAP was putting up a furious resistance.

In the boiler room of the Chancellery, seven men could not believe they were still alive. Minister Briones, who had thought of taking refuge in the Chancellery offices, saw that all that remained of them was an inferno of smoke and flames, but in the boiler room, they were all unharmed. They did not know anything of the president and his group.

Headed by Allende, those who had survived the bombing and the fire in the Moneda returned to the second floor from the cellar and prepared to resist the impending attack of the tanks and infantry. The bombing, they realized, was only the first stage of the war of attrition, the purpose of which was to force Allende to admit the junta's legal authority.

Even now, Briones felt, Allende apparently clung to one idea which he was sure would leave both his life and his government intact. He thought that his three ministers, Almeyda, Briones, and Toha, had succeeded in escaping from the palace before the bombing and must now be negotiating with the representatives of the junta in the Ministry of Defense.

"They still haven't returned. What could have happened to them?" the president repeated.

At that very moment his three ministers and the small group that had taken refuge in the Ministry of Foreign Relations' boiler room had found an intercom connected to the Ministry of Defense still in working condition. After many desperate attempts, they finally were able to speak with General Pinochet's aide: "We are in the Ministry of Foreign Relations: Carlos Briones, Clodomiro Almeyda, Jaime and José Toha, Anibal Palma, Ernesto Espinoza, and another official. We want to get out of here."

"We'll send you a military vehicle."

But the minutes passed, and the vehicle did not appear. More attempts were made to get in touch with the Ministry of Defense. Finally they were answered: "It is impossible to send you a military vehicle. The skirmish is too intense, and we would only risk the lives of both those in the car and yourselves."

Allende asked again, "Why don't they come back? What could have happened?"

The fire in the north wing caused by the bombing continued to grow. The smoke column was visible all over Santiago. The leaders of the Christian Democratic Party were standing on the balcony of the party's emergency hiding place. They had viewed with consternation the eight flyovers of the Hawker Hunters and the burning Moneda, but what could they do now? Their only role would be that of a sorry spectator. Half an hour before, the Christian Democrats' vice-president, Senator Olguin, had called the commander in chief of the army to plead for Allende's life.

He was answered, "We have no intention of taking Allende's life. The matter is entirely in his hands."

Eduardo Frei, the Christian Democrat who had been president before Allende, had also appealed to the junta and had received the same answer.

The Christian Democratic Party could only continue to watch from the terrace.

Santiago was treated to another sensation. At 1230 the Hawker Hunters swooped down on Tomas Moro, in a few instants transforming it into another bonfire. In the bonfire in the center of Santiago was Salvador Allende; in the bonfire in the Alto quarter of Santiago was his wife.

Hortensia Bussi de Allende was lying flat on the floor, trapped between bombs and bullets. She continued to urge the GAP to stop firing on the army which was besieging the house, but the GAP paid no attention, and the Moneda, which she called continuously, did not answer.

The junta had placed General Javier Palacios, Director of Army Instructions, in charge of the ground attack on the Moneda if Allende should refuse to surrender. As the president continued to hold his ground and gave no sign of surrendering, even after the bombing had reduced the Moneda to flames, General Palacios was ordered at 1250 to begin the assault.

The tank battalion of the Second Tank Regiment made the first move. It was operating with a minimal amount of equipment to maintain its mobility in a relatively small area.

The Sherman tanks lined up in Augustin Avenue, trained their cannons on that part of which the north facade of Moneda had been left undamaged by the bombs. Across Constitution Plaza, cannon shots rang out, and the walls crumbled.

Machine gun, rufle, pistol fire answered the cannon fire. The Infantry School, the Petty Officers School, and part of the Tacna Regiment received orders to advance along the four sides of the building. Those who advanced along the north wing were held back by the flames, redoubled by the cannon fire. General Palacios advanced toward the eastern side along Morande Avenue, where it was thought Allende was to be found. It was Palacios's specific and personal mission to capture the president.

On the south facade of the building the infantry's advance was complicated by an unforeseen obstacle: the excavations of the subway under construction. The infantry forces had to cross a narrow wooden bridge, and became perfect targets for the defenders of the south facade, where the Ministry of Foreign Relations was located. However, the artillery found a solution to this problem.

In the Moneda, Allende was shooting his submachine gun from different windows of the palace. His hands were black from gunpowder. Oscar Soto, his personal physician, saw him pick up a bazooka and shoot at an approaching tank, but was not sure whether he had hit his mark. He thought it likely, on the other hand, since he knew that Allende was an excellent marksman. He had observed him handily defeat Fidel Castro in a shooting competition arranged on a cruise along the canals of the deep south, when the Cuban president had visited Chile the year before.

Dr. Soto counted only 18 or 20 GAP remaining alive from a total of 35 who had begun the defense of the Moneda.

The situation could not be more desperate. Allende had to

face up to the fact that his three ministers would not be able to negotiate his continuation in office with the junta, but he had no desire to surrender unconditionally. According to Briones, his plan was to keep up resistance until he could achieve an agreement with the junta which would include the following conditions: an immediate cease-fire, the inclusion in the junta of a civilian acceptable to both Allende and the military men, and a guarantee that the workers who supported him would not be bombed.

Allende would resign under these conditions, but the Ministry of Defense was no longer answering its telephones and to go out on the street was tantamount to suicide.

Hortensia Bussi de Allende's situation was hardly better than her husband's. The furious fight between the GAP and the army was still going on. However, taking advantage of a pause in the skirmish, Carlos Tello, Hortensia's chauffeur, got inside the residence and managed to get her away. He walked with her through the outbuildings of the Convent of the Sacred Heart, a boarding school near the presidential residence, and by car conveyed her to the house of Felipe Herrera, head of the International Development Bank. There the Mexican Ambassador met her and took her to his embassy and safety.

The Tomas Moro residence was deserted. The army had withdrawn to give the bombers room. When the planes had left and before the soldiers returned, the GAP had seized the opportunity to flee.

The bombs had reduced the mansion to a shambles. All the windows were shattered, the walls cracked, the doors unhinged, the furniture in bits and pieces. All kinds of objects were scattered on the floor: radios, record players, televisions, ladies and men's jewelry, pictures, cameras, movie projectors, knick knacks.

EVENTS

In the middle of the unexpected silence, suddenly there was a new invasion. It was not the soldiers returning, not the GAP. This time it was an invasion of the president's neighbors, his less well-off neighbors.

They came by the dozens, men, women, and children. It was not sympathy or solidarity that prompted them to pour into the home of their president. They came only to loot.

The looting was an efficient operation. They did not have much time before the soldiers came back. A human conveyor belt was organized: the entire contents of the mansion passed along it and into a van parked outside. A handful of honest neighbors tried to prevent the ransacking, but no one listened. The loot was too intoxicating.

By the time the soldiers returned, the house had been cleaned out. All that remained was the GAP's abandoned arsenal: anti-tank missiles, heavy and light submachine guns, grenades, and bombs. To the looters, the clothes, the food, the dinner sets, the chandeliers, the electric appliances had been more attractive.

The Final Assault

1200

Laura Allende, the president's sister, arrived at Tomas Moro just after the soldiers. Frustrated in her attempts to reach the Moneda, she had decided to join her sister-in-law. She found the residence surrounded by the army. Oblivious of the danger of being recognized, she asked to be let in, thinking her sister-in-law was still inside, but she was not allowed to enter.

A neighbor who had recognized her approached her and whispered, "Senora Laura, get away from here. They will arrest you. Come to my house if you wish."

"I want to go in. I want to know what has happened." answered Laura, on the verge of tears at the sight of the devastated house.

"First there was the battle between the GAP and the army," the neighbor said. "Then came the bombing. Mrs. Allende was able to escape by car through the rear of the house. Then the looters came. There is no one inside now. It would be better if you leave, Senora Laura."

In a daze, she obeyed him, returned to her car, and drove off.

She did not know where to go or what to do. She was alone. She resumed her pilgrimage in her small vehicle. She moved from one chaotic scene of destruction to another.

Memories of happier days brought tears to her eyes. Two days before, a Sunday, she had had breakfast with her brother at Tomas Moro. She had gone to visit him that morning because of a foreboding. She had had nothing special to say to him, only this strange desire to be near him.

Salvador had been particularly pleased to see her since Laura was still convalescing from an operation. They had a nice big dessert. In the swimming pool were a few little girls, children of friends. Hortensia was returning from Mexico that same afternoon. Everything was normal. Salvador appeared not to share her inexplicable fear.

After lunch he told her he was going to rest a little since he felt very tired, but Laura, still under a spell, could not say goodbye and accompanied him to his room.

Salvador laughed, lay down on his bed, and looked at her. "Well," he said, finally, "give me a kiss and then go because I have to rest. I'm going to pick Hortensia up at the airport."

But Laura was unable to resist the force that obliged her to remain with him. She looked at her brother for a long time and suddenly started to cry.

"My little Laura, why are you crying?"

"I don't know. I am so unhappy, I feel so worried."

"But why? What is happening to you?"

"I have no idea. I am afraid something is going to happen to you."

"What could happen to me?"

"I don't know. I am afraid someone is going to do something to you. I don't want anything to happen to you."

"Laura, what more can happen to me in my life? I am president. I have done my utmost to keep my promises. I have accomplished my goal in life. What more can I ask for? What does it matter what is going to happen to me. Go. Go in peace."

Laura did not answer. She bent over him, kissed him on the forehead, and then left. But a quarter of an hour after she had left Tomas Moro she again felt that irresistible urge to go back to him. She returned to the house, no longer able to hold back her tears. Only a half an hour had elapsed, yet she found Salvador up and in his car ready to go to the airport to fetch his wife. He called her. Laura left her car and approached his.

"Laurita, come with me. Let's go together to wait for Tencha."

But Laura could only look at him in silence. She looked at him and cried.

"How strange!" Salvador said. Then he suggested she wait in the house. They could talk when he returned from the airport.

Laura entered the house and shut herself up in her brother's study. Again she burst into tears.

A maid offered her some coffee. "Senora Laura, what is the matter?"

"I don't know. I am so unhappy."

Soon the wife of Defense Minister Orlando Letelier arrived, and Laura had to fix her face a little to receive her. A little later, Salvador and Hortensia arrived from the airport. Laura had to exert a tremendous effort to keep up a conversation. Suddenly Salvador stood up and said, "Come Laurita."

When they were alone in his study he invited her to sit down, pushed a chair next to hers, and sat down himself. Holding her hand he asked her, "Tell me then, why all this anguish?"

"I don't know. It must be because I see so little of you. Everytime I am able to see you there are always too many people around, and I can't even get near you. It must be because

I haven't seen you for some time on account of my illness. It must be that I see very little of you. . . ."

"But Laurita, don't you know that I love you very much, and if I can't see you often it is because I have a lot of problems?"

"That is what I want you to explain to me!" said Laura in great excitement. "Tell me what is really going on. Tell me if the situation is really, really as serious as everyone has said."

Salvador slowly nodded his head. "I'm afraid it is, and the worst thing is all the obstacles in my way. I try to fix things up and try to reach an understanding, and they mess up everything I do."

He told her the tremendous struggle it had been for him to keep within a legal system while trying to effect fundamental changes in the country's institutions; of his equally great struggle against the pressure from the Left to accelerate progress. Congresswoman Allende herself had exerted such pressures on many occasions, since like many of her colleagues she was convinced that the more the program was accelerated, the sooner Chile would reach the ideal dreamed by all. Laura was finally able to understand her brother's agonizing position, caught between the factions of the parties in the Popular Unity while trying to keep Chile on the road to socialism.

She understood that Salvador was already quite certain he could not continue in this way.

"Laurita, you must understand me. I am not an irresponsible person. I don't want a civil war. I cannot allow an armed confrontation to break out. Chile is divided, her families are divided. Our own family, for example, our own nephew is with the opposition. Just think of all those workers who might die in a civil war. No Laurita, I am not irresponsible."

Relentlessly these memories came back to disturb Congresswoman Allende as she wandered through the chaotic streets of the capital.

How mistaken those were who had believed her brother would call on the workers to defend the Moneda or resist in their factories and towns!

Allende felt the seed of socialism had been sown and that civil war was therefore unnecessary.

Their mother had influenced Salvador a great deal.

"My mother was a woman who behaved differently from other women. When my father became quite ill, she took charge of his law office in Valparaíso, although she had never before worked outside the home. People trusted her, just like they would a professional, so much so that my father had only to check the documents and sign them.

"Salvador loved her very much and felt very proud when she, already an old woman, accompanied him to vote in the elections. She was very erect and very beautiful, and when they walked down the street arm in arm, Salvador felt triumphant. Always she had backed him in his political struggles, whatever the personal cost.

"In the 1958 presidential campaign, for instance, when she was already eighty years old, she received threatening phone calls constantly, but she knew Salvador was fighting for the people and against their suppressors, and did not complain. One day during that campaign when the family was gathered around the dining table, someone told Salvador, 'You could be president of Chile if you would only separate yourself from the Communist party, which is so controversial.'

"Before Salvador could reply, my mother, a deeply religious woman who belonged to the Third Order of the Carmelites, declared, 'Salvador, you should not leave the Communist party. It has been loyal to you and to leave it now would be treason.'

"Salvador has always been loyal. There is no doubt that if he had belonged to another party, to the Radical Party for example, like our father did, he would have been elected president long before 1970.

"But he believed that only socialism could give happiness and justice to the people. When at last he was elected president, he told me, 'How I wish I could enter the Moneda on the arm of my mother.'

"Instead, he entered the Moneda on the arm of his 'Mama Rosa' who took care of him when he was a baby and who had given him the nickname 'Chicho.'

"After the inauguration, the president of the Senate went up to Mama Rosa to congratulate her, and she told him, 'I am very pleased that you could come too, senor.'

" 'Without me, there would be no inauguration, senora,' he replied, and we all burst out laughing.

"You see Salvador really had two mothers."

Laura Allende began to weep as she drove her car through this terrible new world. Suddenly she saw a young man signaling her to stop.

The urgent need to be near another human being made her forget the danger that could result. She invited him to get in.

They were soon chatting. The young man held his head with both hands and suddenly exclaimed, "How terrible! A military government!"

Laura looked at him and said, "I am Laura Allende."

The young man was astonished. "And alone." Impulsively, he put his arms around her shoulders and added, "I am not going to leave you alone. I will stay with you. I want to accompany you."

And so, accompanied by a stranger, Laura Allende went to her own home, where she found no one. Certain that at any moment she would be arrested, she started to put a few things in a suitcase.

General Palacios continued to assault the Moneda using a pincer movement to engage all the forces under his command. The fire from snipers continued. From the Moneda, the president and his supporters kept up a continuous rain of bullets.

General Palacios's forces had been fighting now for more than a half an hour but were still unable to enter the Moneda. It was 1330.

General Palacios decided to divide his personal command and lead one group along Augustin Avenue to Bandera Avenue, then advance to Moneda Avenue. They quickly arrived, shoulders plastered against the wall, at the corner of Morande Avenue and the Administration offices. It cost him fifteen wounded and two dead to achieve this position, but he was in sight of his objective: the door of 80 Morande Avenue.

Reacting to the continued resistance of the Moneda, General Baeza, liaison between the junta and the army staff, proposed using tear gas to force unconditional surrender without losing any more men.

The carabineros were charged with this operation. When they finished, the Moneda was drowning in a sea of gas, which made it impossible to see, and explosions, which made it impossible to hear.

Allende decided to send his chief adviser on internal affairs, Fernando Flores, his undersecretary of the interior, Daniel Vergara, and his private secretary, Osvaldo Puccio, to the Defense Ministry to reiterate his conditions for relinquishing his office.

The three delegates left the palace with their hands up. A contingent from General Palacios's forces escorted them safely to the Ministry of Defense. In the Moneda the shooting continued.

In the second floor office overlooking Morande Avenue, Dr. Patricio Guijon, watched Augusto Olivares approach Allende.

"Any news yet?" asked the president.

Olivares shook his head.

"We are lost. We have no friends in the armed forces."

"Then we have no other choice but surrender," said Allende. "Let's tell the Ministry of Defense."

On the fifth floor of the Ministry of Defense the three presidential delegates had met with a categorical refusal from the chief of staff, vice-admiral Carvajal. He had been instructed by the junta to demand the surrender of the president, conceding only the sparing of his life.

At that moment the intercom from the Moneda rang and the vice-admiral's secretary answered it. Colonel Pedro Ewing did not recognize the voice.

"Has Daniel Vergara arrived?"

"Yes, with Puccio and Flores."

"Have they reached any agreement?"

"There is nothing to agree to except unconditional surrender."

"Will Vergara, Puccio, and Flores come back to the Moneda?"

"No."

"Thanks," the voice answered, and the connection was broken.

A few minutes later, a spokesman from the Moneda announced over the intercom that all those inside had surrendered and were starting to leave the palace.

The three delegates were placed under arrest with one of Osvaldo Puccio's sons who had accompanied his father.

The man who had spoken to Colonel Ewing was Augusto Olivares. He told Allende about the failure of the three delegates, then went down to a bathroom under the staircase which led to the kitchen. Without bothering to close the door, he started to urinate. At that moment Oscar Soto was passing. Bitter jokes were exchanged. Then Dr. Soto continued upstairs. A few minutes later he heard a shot. He ran back to the bathroom. Olivares had shot himself with a revolver.

Carlos Jorquera, the presidential attaché, when he saw the body of his friend and colleague, started to cry bitterly.

For Salvador Allende the suicide of his closest collaborator represented a heavy blow.

What else could be done but submit to the will of the junta? Or was there another way out, such as that taken by Augusto Olivares?

In the Ministry of Defense, orders had been given to cease fire around the Moneda as soon as word had been received that Allende was unconditionally surrendering. An armored vehicle with a patrol headed by an officer of the army started out toward the Moneda but immediately came under fire from the remaining snipers.

The patrol was forced to turn back and was not able to accomplish its mission of transporting the president to the Ministry of Defense.

General Palacios and his command waited in front of the evacuated Offices of Administration. The faces of his officers, down to his youngest recruits, had lost the pallor that had been on their faces during the first five or ten minutes of the cross fire. They seemed perfectly intent on their objective: to enter the Moneda.

These soldiers had been protecting their general with their own bodies. If the butt of a machine gun appeared at a window, they got him out of the line of fire. A single look was sufficient for them to understand his orders and execute them.

The general was deeply impressed and touched by the conduct of his men during the supreme test of a soldier: action in the face of the enemy.

For General Palacios, the moment of truth had arrived. It was time to enter the Moneda and take charge of the "gentleman," as he called Allende.

He requested covering fire from the surrounding tanks and advanced under a rain of bullets to the door on Morande Avenue.

The tanks circled, stopped, withdrew, and then resumed their advance. The noise was deafening.

Before reaching the door, General Palacios saw a white doctor's coat hung from one of the balconies of the Moneda as a sign of surrender. At that very instant, inside the Moneda a group of about thirty people including members of the GAP, the National Bureau of Investigations, and doctors was approaching the same door that the general was trying to break down.

They had come down from the second floor to give themselves up. Among them was Dr. Soto, who had put down his submachine gun and was talking to one of his colleagues when the door to the street suddenly collapsed and a platoon of soldiers with red bandannas around their necks charged in. At their head was a bespectacled commander whose right lens had been shattered.

"Surrender you bastards, all of you!" roared the commander.

Together with the others, Oscar Soto was pushed against a wall, his arms raised.

But when shots were heard from the second floor, the commander shouted, "Everybody down on the ground, face down!"

They followed the order as quickly as they could, and the laggards received encouragement from the butts of rifles.

General Palacios started to count his prisoners, and then suddenly exclaimed, "What's this?"

He had found a woman in the group.

He looked amazed, for he was certain that all the women had left the Moneda during the truce that Allende had called for that very purpose, and he ordered her to get up.

An officer whispered in his ear, "That's the president's secretary, sir."

But this fact made no impression on him. General Palacios had just returned from two years in Germany a few months before, and it did not occur to him to associate Allende's secretary with the famous "La Payita."

He was much more concerned that the lady in question had been seized by an attack of hysterics; she was jumping, twisting, and screaming to such an extent that the general ordered an ambulance be summoned immediately to take her to the military hospital.

Dr. Soto, who was also lying face down on the ground, heard the general say to him, "And you, sir, what are you doing here?"

Oscar Soto attributed the officer's more formal form of address to the difference in his appearance from the other prisoners', for he was still wearing his blue suit, white shirt, and tie. He also noted that the prisoners received much better treatment at the hands of this and the other officers than what the troops were handing out. The latter would take every opportunity to deal out blows, insults and thwacks with their rifles or machine guns.

The atmosphere in the Moneda was hardly calm; the eyes of both the soldiers and the civilians were reddened and weeping from the tear gas. The smoke, the flames, and the falling, blazing beams threatened to engulf them. Outside and inside the enclosed area, the clamor of combat continued.

Dr. Soto heard the general saying to him, "Go up to the

second floor and tell Allende that he has ten minutes left to surrender. Tell him and everyone else up there to come down unarmed and with their hands up."

Dr. Soto obeyed and went up to the second floor.

There he found Allende, still helmeted and carrying his machine gun, but without his jacket, dispensing orders left and right. When Oscar Soto approached him and informed him that he and the remaining GAPs had ten minutes to go downstairs, unarmed and with their arms raised, Allende seemed not to hear him.

Instead, he watched a battle of unusual intensity that had just broken out in the next building, which housed the Ministry of Public Works. At last he said, as if from another world, "Go down, go down all of you. I shall go down last of all."

Oscar Soto returned to the ground floor, where he was immediately seized by troops (there were no longer any officers in sight) and was pushed outside the enclosure. Dealing him blows with their rifle butts, they forced him to lie, face downward, on the pavement.

An ambulance of the National Health Service was waiting in the vicinity of the Moneda. Its staff was attached to the government and had been cautiously waiting for the opportunity to come to the aid of those defending the palace. Suddenly, the ambulance pulled away, stopped before the door of 80 Morande Avenue, and quickly took on board the woman handed over by a soldier who thought he was following the general's orders. The ambulance drove away just as quickly as it had approached, but it was not heading for the military hospital.

Inside the ambulance, La Payita had suddenly recovered from her hysterics. She was being carried away, far from the Moneda now in flames, far from the center of Santiago, leaving behind her comrade president, at whose side she had wished to remain right up to the very last moment, no matter what the sacrifice.

The ten minutes that General Palacios had allowed Allende expired without his surrender. Since shots were still being fired from the second floor, the general went up, accompanied by a few men, in order to bring the "gentleman" out personally.

But this final part of his mission was to prove very difficult.

As he reached the Presidential Gallery, lined with marble busts depicting all the presidents in the history of the Chilean Republic, General Palacios realized that the worst part of his task was just beginning. Seven or eight GAPs were still putting up a proud and desperate resistance. As the fire advanced upon them from the rear with devastating rapidity, these GAPs either fell, riddled with bullets, or perished in the fire, but those who remained alive would not surrender.

As the soldiers approached from the other end of the Presidential Gallery, the GAPs defended every room, fired their machine guns from every doorway. Two more soldiers dropped dead in the fray.

General Palacios, moving from room to room toward his objective, turned suddenly into the gallery to find himself face to face with a GAP—a boy no more than eighteen years old—who was standing just a few steps away, his machine gun trained on the general.

The boy fired, missed, and before he could fire again, Lieutenant Fernandez rushed up, catching a bullet in his arm, before shooting the boy in the head, emptying his whole magazine.

One of the bullets ricocheted off the boy's steel helmet and lodged in the general's hand.

The lieutenant promptly offered a handkerchief to his superior, whose hand had begun to bleed profusely from a ruptured vein.

"Thank you, lieutenant."

They then resumed their advance toward the presidential offices. The general was certain that was where he would find his final objective.

In the Presidential Gallery, the marble busts of the past presidents of Chile were being blasted to smithereens as they were shattered by the bullets of one side or the other. The soldiers left behind, sitting on the ground, a GAP whose body had stopped eleven bullets. General Palacios asked him for his papers and questioned him:

"And you, where are you from?"

"From the South."

"And what are you doing here, kid?"

"My comrades brought me here. They told me they'd give me a land lot."

"They sure have landed you in a fine lot, you idiot! Just look at the fix you're in now!"

The GAPs were just a few yards away, darting from room to room, poking their heads around the doorways as they fired, continuously shouting to each other to keep their courage up. References to the soldiers' parentage, genitals, and rear ends reverberated with the bullet shots from one side to the other.

When the general reached the O'Higgins Hall it was already in flames.

"This is an historical monument! Try to save the antiques!" shouted General Palacios, as he rolled up carpets and took down drapes to save them from the flames.

"Pick up those machine guns and take them downstairs!"

Weapons were hanging everywhere: machine guns, rifles, grenades, gas masks, helmets. From time to time, explosions could be heard when a crate of ammunition caught fire. Apart from the president, General Palacios's greatest preoccupation, he confided afterward, was to save the O'Higgins saber, which he finally managed to seize hold of and send downstairs for safe-keeping.

The advance continued toward the final objective in groups of three: one running forward while the other kept him covered by cross fire.

"Now let's get that room on the right!"

"Watch out! There's another son of a bitch!"

"Shoot him, you idiot!"

"You run over and stay by that door, I'll keep you covered."

"There he goes, there he goes!"

"Let him have it! Don't let him get away!"

"How many are there left?"

The general calculated: the Tomas Moro GAPs fled like rats after the bombing; Allende telephoned them to tell them to come to the Moneda, but not one of them had obeyed his orders. Out of the thirty or so in the Moneda, two have surrendered and are downstairs; some others died in the flames. There can be no more than four or five left—the best and most loyal ones; of these, two have already been sent to the hospital, one with seven bullets, the other with eleven. . . .

As an admirer of the heroic virtues, the general was disillusioned by the GAPs. Except for a handful who had resisted with true fanaticism, neither giving nor begging for quarter, the others had displayed a training fit for amateurs: they were overconfident of their own strength but incapable of fighting as a team. . . .

The roof began to cave in and was gradually enveloped in the flames. General Palacios's group was joined by the other soldiers who had been advancing from the other end of La Moneda. The two jaws of the pincers had met.

An officer shouted, "Over here, General! In Independence Hall! Come quickly!"

The Death of Allende

1430

Meanwhile, the junta continued its broadcasts to the country over the radio network without opposition.

Whereas:

One—Allende's government has committed grave infractions of the law by violating the fundamental rights of freedom of speech, freedom of instruction, the right to strike, the right to petition, the right of ownership and, in general, the right to a dignified and assured subsistence.

Two—the same government has fractured the national unity by artificially fomenting a futile, and in many cases bloody, class struggle, losing the valiant support of all Chileans who could contribute to the good of the country, and bringing about a fratricidal and blind struggle between ideas that are false, alien to our way of life, and doomed to failure.

Three—that the same government has shown itself to be incapable of assuring peace amongst Chileans by neither respecting the law nor seeing that it be respected, and thus gravely violating the law on repeated occasions.

Four—furthermore, the government has placed itself above the constitution on numerous occasions by adopting dubious resolutions and distorted and self-serving interpretations, or, on other occasions flagrantly adopting those that, for various reasons, have remained unsanctioned.

Five—moreover, by using subterfuge which they themselves have classified as "legal loopholes," they have left some laws unexecuted and have violated others, thus creating situations that have in fact been illegal right from their inception.

Six—it has also repeatedly flouted the mutual respect that the state powers must maintain toward each other, by disregarding the decisions of the National Congress, the Judiciary, and the Department of the Treasury of the Republic [a suprajudicial body with the authority to arbitrate between the Presidency, the Congress, and the Judiciary], issuing inadmissable excuses or simply no explanation at all.

Seven—the Executive has overstepped its powers in a deliberate and flagrant manner by attempting to accumulate in its own hands the greatest degree of political and economic power to the detriment of vital national activities, and by gravely jeopardizing all the rights and freedoms of this country's citizens.

Eight—the president of the republic has publicly shown the country that his personal authority is influenced by the decisions of committees and directives of political parties and groups supporting him, thus losing the image of maximum authority bestowed upon him by the Constitution, and consequently the presidential character of the government.

Nine—that the agricultural, commercial, and industrial economy of the country is in a stagnant or recessive condition, and inflation is rapidly increasing, without any sign in sight as to any concern for these problems which the government, apparently acting as a mere spectator of the crisis, is allowing to run rampant.

Ten—anarchy, the suffocation of freedoms, and moral and economic upheaval are present throughout the country, and a situation of absolute irresponsibility or inefficiency exists within the government, causing the situation in Chile to deteriorate and denying her her rightful place as one of the foremost nations on the continent.

Eleven—all of the above, contained in the preceding paragraphs, are sufficient to conclude that the internal and external security of the country is in danger, that the existence of our independent state is in jeopardy, and that the maintenance of the government is detrimental to the best interests of the republic and of its sovereign people.

Twelve—these same antecedents are, in the light of the classical doctrine which typifies our historic thought, sufficient to justify our intervention in deposing the illegitimate and immoral government which does not represent the great national sentiment, thus avoiding those greater evils which the present power vacuum might bring about, for there are no other reasonably effective measures to achieve this end, it being our purpose to reestablish economic and social normalcy throughout the country, and to regain the peace, tranquility and security that have been lost.

Thirteen—for all the reasons briefly expressed above, the armed forces have assumed the moral duty imposed upon them by the fatherland to dismiss the government which, although initially legitimate, has fallen into flagrant illegality, and to assume such power by reason of the circumstances which require said assumption, supported by the evidence of the sentiment of the large majority of the population, this sentiment being in its own right, before God and on behalf of posterity, the justification for such action, and, ultimately, for the resolutions, norms, and instructions that become necessary in order to accomplish the task it has committed itself to fulfil, for the common good and in the best interests of the fatherland.

Fourteen—therefore, these norms shall be observed and complied with by the whole country and above all by the authorities.

Signed: The Junta Government of the Chilean Armed
Forces and Carabineros. Santiago, September 11, 1973.

"General! In Independence Hall!"

General Palacios ran in the direction pointed out to him by
the officer and, helped by three men, managed to open the door.

He found himself in a room that was almost intact, furnished
in red plush and an enormous picture depicting the Oath of
Independence. Leaning back in the red armchair, his head
slightly tilted over his shoulder, was a man whose face at first
sight was unrecognizable.

His hands were swollen and covered in dust. Around him, on
the ground, were empty submachine gun shells. On the sofa were
a steel helmet and a gas mask. He was wearing reddish brown
trousers, a gray pullover, and a tweed jacket. Strangely enough,
his shoes were clean.

"This must be the gentleman," thought General Palacios,
and he asked the man he had found next to the corpse, "Is this
Allende?"

"Yes, general sir, it is."

"You're lying."

The general then looked more closely. There was not a single
spot of blood, just his brains spattered all over him. A bullet hole
could be seen in the tapestry covering the wall. The shot must
have been fired a few moments before.

On his wrist was a handsome blue watch which the general
recognized from the few times that he had seen the president.
Leaning against the body was the submachine gun received from
Fidel Castro as a gift.

The general turned toward the other man and looked at him,
"And who are you, young man?"

The other man identified himself: Patricio Guijon, the president's physician.

He was very pale. He recounted how Allende had ordered them all to go downstairs and surrender, saying that he would go down last of all, upon which he closed the door of Independence Hall and remained alone.

"I was going downstairs," said the doctor, "deathly afraid, for we were sure that they were going to kill us all down there. I have never handled a weapon in my life, I was here as a doctor. I suddenly heard two shots, turned around, opened the door, and saw President Allende's body slumped in the armchair."

"And what did you do?"

"The first thing that occurred to me was to attend to his injuries, but right away I realized there was no point. I took the submachine gun and stood it up again."

"And you didn't touch anything else?"

"Nothing else."

The general continued to question him. Allende had apparently seemed very sure of himself at the beginning, but the disillusionments quickly followed each other: first the withdrawal of the carabinero reinforcements with their tanks; then the withdrawal of the palace guard; the capture of the GAP with the heavy armaments; the irrefutable evidence that he could count on no one in the armed forces; the air raid; the firing of the tank cannons; the suicide of Olivares.

"They have tricked me!" exclaimed Allende, according to Guijon's account.

General Palacios realized that the situation was a compromising one, and his reaction was prompt. He called a guard.

"No one is to come in!"

Downstairs two German and two Dutch reporters had already arrived. They were only allowed to photograph the arsenal that had been discovered in the Moneda.

General Palacios ordered that firemen be summoned to isolate the hall to avoid a fire that might incinerate the "gentle-man," leaving no proof of what had occurred.

The firemen complied.

The only room that remained intact in the burning palace was Independence Hall.

General Palacios then radioed to General Herman Brady, in charge of the Santiago plan.

"Mission accomplished. Moneda taken. President dead."

He did not use the word "suicide."

First of all, he was still not totally convinced that the body was Allende's. In the second place, it was also quite probable that some GAP had taken it upon himself to assassinate him, al-though, reflected the general, the trajectory of the bullet made that unlikely. Only an idiot would have chosen to shoot from below the chin and run the risk of merely wounding him or shooting his eye out. If you want to kill, you shoot through the heart.

To dispel all doubt, General Palacios summoned the Foren-sic Division of the Homicide Squad, a politic choice because, in his opinion, the division had been infiltrated by the Popular Unity. They arrived at 1630.

Inspector Pedro Espinoze was the head of the Homicide Squad group, which included Detective Julio Navarro, the bal-listics experts Jorge Almanzabal and Carlos Davison, the sur-veyor Alejandro Ossandon, the forensic photographer Enrique Contreras, and the impressions expert Hector Henriquez. They confirmed on the spot General Palacios's supposition that Al-lende had killed himself.

Later, they submitted a written report.

An external examination by the police revealed in the chin a star-shaped erosive-contused wound, representing the point of entry of the projectile, and on the borders of which was an appreciable amount of carbonaceous dust. In the right superficial zygomatic arch, another wound, apparently the point of exit of the projectile or of a bone splinter. In the left parietal region, a wound marking the bullet's point of exit producing the shattering of the cranial vault. There are fractures in the upper jaw, maxillary, the lower maxillary, the nose, and the forehead. Lividity developing in the corresponding areas. Incipient rigidity at the maxillary level. Probable cause of death: Cranial-encephalic trauma from a bullet wound of a suicidal nature.

No wound was noted other than those mentioned.

Back at the Moneda, his doubts dispelled, General Palacios considered the corpse of Allende.

As a soldier, he respected his courage in refusing to surrender, whatever the reasons for committing suicide at the last moment.

There was not much time for pondering. The firemen were rushing about fighting the blaze, the prisoners and wounded were waiting downstairs, the arms that were scattered all over the place had to be gathered together, the archives and art works had to be saved from the fire, the troops had to be reviewed, the reporters taken care of, and . . . . the "gentleman's" body disposed of.

But these tasks involved other men. General Javier Palacios's special mission was now accomplished.

The Silence

1600

The suburbs of Santiago were quiet, the silence of the streets broken only by motorized patrols of the army and carabineros. In their homes, people kept their ears glued to their radios. They had just listened to communique number ten from the junta, announcing a list of ninety-five persons ordered to present themselves voluntarily at the Ministry of Defense before 4:30 P.M., or become "subject to such measures as shall be deemed necessary by the junta of the commanders in chief, with the easily foreseeable consequences that would be incurred thereby."

The list comprised the entire upper echelon of the Popular Unity Coalition, of which twenty-six members were already at the Ministry of Defense, and many others had sought asylum in various embassies, mainly those of Mexico, Argentina, Sweden, Venezuela, and Colombia.

Those who were still fighting from the rooftops of the Ministry of Public Works and the State Bank, in the Central Bank of Chile, in from the Social Security building, from the offices of the *Clarin* newspaper, or the University of Engineering were not the leaders of the Popular Unity parties.

The snipers fought on valiantly, but those on the rooftops were implacably overpowered by bombing from helicopters, and those shooting from the inside of the building could not defend themselves from bazooka fire.

No apparent resistance occurred in the industrial buildings and factories.

There were many possible reasons for the passivity of the workers during the coup. The flight of their leaders was important, as was their lack of arms or sufficient training to wage an effective struggle. Harder to define but perhaps critical to the coup's quick success was the lack of a mystique surrounding the Popular Unity. Unlike those in Cuba, Chilean workers before Allende were not in a desperate state. Under Allende, their lot undoubtedly improved, but who is ready to die for higher wages? Unfortunately, for many workers it was this attitude which predominated.

Then there was the dispiriting speed of efficiency of the coup's execution. To the workers, it came as a complete surprise. Only in the minds and on the lips of some of the Popular Unity leaders did both the threat and the preparation for a coup exist.

In addition, and largely unknown to the rank and file, the Communist Party in Chile played a role similar to that of the Vatican: they wanted only peace, collaboration, and national unity—because Moscow did not want another problematic expense, such as Cuba had been. Allende himself, aware of all these facts, carefully avoided urging the workers to engage in all out resistance to the coup during his last speech to the nation.

"The people must not sacrifice themselves," he had said. And the people—during these crucial twenty-four hours—did not.

Carlos Briones, waiting in the Ministry of Defence, was impressed with the generals' exemplary courtesy, particularly toward Briones himself.

The ministers, who had been cut off from Allende's group since before the bombing, asked after the president.

"He is dead," said General Nuno, "but not by one of our bullets."

Minister Briones inferred that Allende had killed himself or, like General Palacios, he speculated that the president might have been felled by a GAP's bullet. In silence—for he and his colleagues were forbidden to speak amongst themselves—he waited for the uniformed officials to decide his fate.

The group of detained ministers in the Ministry of Defense was soon joined by Daniel Vergara, Osvaldo Puccio, and Fernando Flores.

A colonel of the Military Intelligence questioned them. Briones was surprised that the interrogation ended up in a most amiable discussion on politics in general.

They would be transferred to the Military Academy, the colonel informed them, where they would be treated with all the respect due their rank.

"Now you are under the army's protection," he said.

He left them in a room, with the continued injunction against speaking with one another. For Briones, this was the most difficult restriction he had to endure while he was in the Ministry of Defense, for everyone was anxious to give and receive news.

They could still hear the clamor of the siege that was going on in the buildings around the Moneda. But no one spoke.

After a medical inspection they were transferred by bus to the Military Academy and lodged in the lieutenants' quarters. "And very well taken care of," added Minister Briones.

Laura Allende's Brother

1630

Just as Congresswoman Laura Allende was again leaving her house to look for a safer place, one of her nephews arrived and persuaded her to go to his house.

Laura decided to follow him, although he was a member of the main opposition party to Allende's government—the Christian Democrats—because "family ties are far stronger than political differences."

She remained in her nephew's home until she heard her name was one of the ninety-five on the wanted list, broadcast by the junta over the radio.

She decided to move to the house of a friend not related to her in any way and stayed there, her ear tuned to the radio and telephone, trying to find out the fate of her brother Salvador.

At a late hour, a doctor friend at the San Borja Hospital confirmed the president's death. But the words seemed to mean hardly anything to her: the past still refused to step aside and make way for today's somber avalanche of events.

Comrade Allende—I liked so much to call him "Comrade Allende"—had his faults. But he himself would laugh and say: "I am just like any other of our comrades." When he spoke to the townspeople and peasants, he would say, "I like to enjoy a good meal, too. I enjoy a good drink, and I like to have a good time when I feel like it, have fun . . . "

But when he was president, we could never have any fun, for I used to find him constantly working.

Comrade President was also a man who would easily lose his patience, most of all with slow, fussy people who would take up his time talking about petty problems. This impatience of his used to upset many people when he would cut them short: "Yes, yes, yes," he would say, "I get the point. I'll see what I can do."

He was a lonely man, with never a moment for relaxation. This would create a distance between himself and other people. Anyone who wanted to keep up a lengthy conversation with him felt frustrated.

He was a great friend of Fidel Castro, whom he admired just as we all admire him. Many times, before he was president, when he had to go on a trip, he would go by way of Cuba. He would spend two or three days at Varaderos, fishing and chatting with Fidel.

He also had friends who were always at his side, like Augusto Olivares, whom he would talk to for hours, not about himself, but about national problems.

Salvador was a man without hate. I never heard him speak indignantly or spitefully about anyone. But he did have deep dislikes, such as those he harbored for the newspaper *El Mercurio* [a stronghold of Far Right intellectuals].

On various occasions, when Salvador knew that someone had been inefficient and he asked that he be dismissed from his job, I used to hear him say, "That comrade was not ready for this transition." And I believe that some were really not ready, for the transition demanded changes in the individual himself,

101

which often could not be realized because the external events occurred far more rapidly than the internal or personal ones.

People were asked to change their mentality, but not everyone did so, not everyone understood the enormous sacrifices that were required, the tremendous efforts, the deep honesty that had to be created. But many did understand, and I believe that what had been done cannot be undone. The man and woman who acquired a degree of personal dignity, the factory worker who acquired a participatory interest that he had never had before, the peasant who organized himself—none of them can turn back, because they now know how to make their demands heard and, sooner or later, will attain the goal that Salvador Allende always proclaimed:

"Everyone must realize his full potential and be part of his Government. Government should be identical with the people, but to achieve this, people must participate in it directly."

Allende's Funeral

1700

General Javier Palacios was standing beside Allende's body. The Homicide Squad had completed its technical examination, and the general covered the body with a Bolivian rug he found in the room. The guards were allowing no one to enter except the firemen and recruits. General Palacios felt a sense of shock at the insults that were being hurled at the corpse, especially by the firemen, who apparently blamed Allende for all that had happened. The recruits seemed more respectful, limiting themselves to staring curiously.

They told jokes to help pass the time. An officer told the joke about the Mexican corporal who said to his commanding officer:

"Captain, I've got twenty escapees here under arrest."

"Then shoot the lot of them!"

Ten minutes later, the corporal returned.

"Captain, I was wrong, they were not escapees, they were refugees."

"You have to keep your sense of humor in battle," the general reflected.

The labor of gathering together the arms and valuable objects continued around him, while the firemen continued to keep the fire away from Independence Hall.

After he had expressed his concern that his men had not had any food since breakfast, the general was told, "Don't worry, general. They are already having lunch."

"What! Where did they get it from?"

"A regular banquet, sir! Whiskey, imported jams, ham, delicacies such as we haven't seen in Chile for years. We were able to save them from the Moneda kitchens before they caught fire. There's no doubt that our friend the president treated himself well."

Down below, the prisoners were waiting to be identified by the Intelligence Service. The general noticed that there was a group around a man who looked particularly pale.

The general, recognizing the prisoner, could not resist a dig. "Weren't you the one who was talking so much about the armed revolution? How come you have nothing to say now?"

The man he addressed was Carlos Jorquera, presidential press attaché, known throughout Chile for his fiery oratory.

The group of doctors attached to the president also received their share of abuse from their captors, which they answered by claiming the proper respect due their profession.

General Palacios replied, "What do you take us for? If you were simply physicians to the president, how come you set up a hospital large enough to accommodate a hundred wounded?"

Later, after they had administered medical care to patients of both sides, Oscar Soto and some of his colleagues, instead of being sent to the Tacna Regiment headquarters together with the other prisoners, were accompanied by an officer to a less dangerous zone where after their documents had been confiscated they were released.

The agents of the Investigation Service in charge of the president's personal security, who had taken part in the defense of the Moneda, also argued their case with General Palacios.

General Palacios was sympathetic. These people were not GAPs, after all. But on the other hand they were not able to dispel his suspicions.

"If you had been in my place, general, you would have done exactly the same," argued one of the agents. "I was simply carrying out orders and had to carry them out right to the bitter end."

"Oh, come on," retorted the general, "why didn't you surrender when you realized that there was no other way? Nothing doing, gentlemen! You are under arrest and shall go to the Tacna!"

General Palacios reserved special treatment for the interior minister, Carlos Briones. When he was informed that Briones had been found in the Ministry of Foreign Relations he ordered that he be treated with particular respect.

"That little old man is a very good person. He had been trying to conciliate the president with the Christian Democrats and despaired because he was not able to. A most sound man. He was secretary to President Alessandri, an expert on social welfare law. He had nothing to do with this."

The ambulance finally arrived, and Allende's body, wrapped in the Bolivian rug, was taken to the Military Hospital.

At exactly five o'clock in the afternoon, the telephone rang at the secret headquarters of the Christian Democratic Party.

Someone calling on behalf of the junta informed the leaders who had gathered there that Salvador Allende had committed suicide.

The party vice-president, Senator Olguin, then suggested that the autopsy be performed by the director of the Institute of Forensic Medicine, Dr. Vargas, in the presence of two Christian Democrat members of Congress. The chief of command raised no objection and promised to call the party back in order to give the address of the place where the autopsy would be performed.

The party leaders waited, but the call from the junta never came. The autopsy was performed in the Military Hospital in the presence of four heads of the medical services of the army, navy, air force, and carabineros.

Eduardo Arriagada, president of the College of Engineers, was looking out of a window of the college building that overlooked the east and south sides of the Moneda, still in flames. He could not help admiring the bravery of Allende, who, finding himself surrounded by only a few GAP—little more than hired gunmen in Arriagada's eyes—was faithful to what he had said that morning.

"I shall resist no matter what, even if it costs me my life."

"Even mediocre people," thought Arriagada, "when pushed to their limits, become admirable."

The deceitful, superficial Allende whom he had known had acted with surprising dignity when confronted with the junta's demands.

"The news of Allende's suicide," he remarked, "left a bitter aftertaste on such a glorious day."

At ten o'clock on the night of the eleventh, in a silent, restrained Valparaíso, Commander Jorge Contreras appeared at the home of the Grove Allende family, with orders from the joint chiefs of staff to inform Salvador Allende's closest relatives in Valparaíso that he had committed suicide and that the junta wished to know in which cemetery of that city they wished him to be buried.

Commander Contreras, who had no idea of how the president's cousins might react, felt somewhat uneasy. However, Mr. Grove was abroad and his wife, while very shocked at the news, pointed out that she had never shared Salvador Allende's ideas, so the interview passed fairly smoothly. As to the burial, she told him that it would have to take place in the Santa Ines Cemetery, where the family tomb was located and where a month previously Ines Allende, Salvador's sister and the mother of Mr. Grove Allende, had been buried.

The next day, September 12, at seven o'clock in the morning, the telephone rang in the Santiago home of a friend of Laura Allende, where the latter had taken refuge.

It was a call from a cousin who had obtained permission from the junta to accompany Salvador Allende's body to the Santa Ines Cemetery in Viña del Mar.

Laura was terrified at the prospect of seeing the corpse of her brother. At the same time, she realized that it was her duty to face reality.

At eight o'clock in the morning, her cousin came to pick her up and together they went to the Military Hospital in the center of Santiago.

A uniformed guard asked them what they wanted. Laura could no longer contain herself, and, in tears, she replied, "I want to see comrade Allende, whom you killed."

Unmoved, the guard stared at her.

"He is not here," he said, "but stay here. I'll ask."

Then a doctor appeared.

"I'm sorry, but we cannot give you any information. Go to the Ministry of Defense."

Upon their arrival at the Ministry of Defense, they were promptly ordered by the guards to get out of the car. The cousin approached the high iron doors and explained that he was accompanying Salvador Allende's sister.

"Laura Allende will have to be detained," they answered him.

The cousin returned to where Laura was waiting for him, but he did not tell her what he had just heard.

They had to run to the entrance to the ministry, for shooting was still going on between the snipers and soldiers. They went up to a room where what appeared to Laura to be a group of generals and admirals was waiting for them. Laura could recognize none of them with certainty.

However, she believed one of them to be the commander in chief of the air force, General Gustavo Leigh Guzman, one of the members of the junta. Laura found she could not extend her hand to any of them. Each time one of the officials made as if to shake her hand, all she could do was look at them and weep. She could not understand how they could have the audacity to shake her hand after the treachery they had committed.

The officers ignored her slight and informed her she was authorized to travel back and forth from Santiago to Viña del Mar in order to accompany her brother's body to the cemetery. There was not the slightest risk of her being arrested, and they had an airplane available, ready to depart for Viña del Mar immediately.

In the military section of Cerrillos Airport, a few miles from Santiago, the casket was already waiting for Laura and her cousin's arrival. Shortly afterward, Hortensia Bussi de Allende arrived and begged to see the body, but she was told the casket was already completely sealed and could not be opened. The airplane then took off, bound for the coast.

The trip beside the coffin was very difficult for Laura. During the journey she came to the realization that because of her brother's death she would never be able to leave Chile.

"I want to stay here and live through what all the other Chileans are living through," she thought to herself. "I want to stay in Chile, because I could never bear to be far away, not knowing what is happening to my fellow citizens, to my co-workers, to the children, to the youth.

"I want to stay here even if all I can do is offer my presence, for my presence is part of the presence of Salvador. I shall move from house to house, but I shall never ask for asylum in any embassy. Once I have recovered from my illness, I am willing to accept any conditions they impose upon me, but I shall not ask for any special treatment. I want to share the life that other Chileans will be leading, the life of my comrades.

"My heart is in Barrancas, in Conchalf, in all the many towns that make up this people, but I don't know if I shall be forced to follow another route."

On the plane traveling with her brother's body to the coast, Laura remembered a night with Salvador at the Caupolican Theater in Santiago.

Allende was at the height of his presidential campaign and was addressing tens of thousands of partisans in the enormous auditorium.

Amongst them was Mama Rosa, who at one point stood up, shouting, "Right on, my son!"

At these words, someone near her retorted, "What do you think your son's going to be, you old fool!"

Mama Rosa looked at him, indignant, and replied in her booming voice, "What do you think? I reared him! And there's no one in Chile smarter than he!"

In Valparaíso, Commander Contreras had gone to pick up

the wife of Grove Allende, and they both proceeded to the Quinteros air naval base. They were the only people meeting the airplane, which landed at 12:05.

The coffin was to be accompanied by Hortensia, Laura, two cousins, Patricio and Eduardo Grove, and a representative of the Ministry of the Interior, Air Commander Sanchez.

As the airplane was approaching, one of the two Grove cousins went up to Commander Contreras and whispered in his ear, "Laura Allende, I am sure, is very upset, so she probably will not come up to say hello to you."

At 12:25, the entire group had reached the Santa Ines Cemetery, now empty and surrounded by armed guards.

"It was so sad," recollected Laura. "We were all by ourselves, and it was all so mysterious, so hurried, as we walked along surrounded by armed guards so that no one would find out what was going on."

Commander Contreras ordered the van carrying the coffin to enter the cemetery and proceed to the site where the navy personnel had had the burial ground prepared. As she arrived at the open grave, Allende's widow approached the commander and told him that in Santiago the military authorities had informed her that she would be allowed to see her husband for the last time at the cemetery.

"Madam," replied the marine, "I'm sorry, but I have not been authorized to allow it. In any case, I believe that the casket is completely sealed."

It was a lead coffin, but when it was moved, it was apparent that the lid was loose, so Commander Contreras decided to permit the lid to be raised and the widow to look at her dead husband through the glass cover.

But all that could been seen of Salvador Allende was his face, entirely swathed in bandages.

The widow then asked that the entire coffin be opened, but

the commander repeated that he did not have the authority and that the coffin seals could not be soldered again once they had been opened.

Hortensia Bussi de Allende apparently decided not to press the point, and the casket was placed in the tomb of the Grove family.

Laura watched the faces of the six men who were lowering the coffin into the crypt and concluded from their expressions that they were unaware of whom they were burying.

"Here lies comrade Allende," she said to them. "The people will not forget him."

Then, according to Commander Contreras, the widow plucked a wild flower and dropped it on the coffin.

"It is an absolute disgrace that the duly elected president of Chile should be buried alone, like a dog," Hortensia declared.

Laura Allende also plucked a wild flower and cast it on the coffin, but it did not hit its mark. One of the workmen went down into the crypt, picked it up, and laid it in its intended place.

Laura noticed the eyes of one of the workmen were filled with tears.

ISSUES

Allende's Death

The president of the Christian Democratic Party, Senator Patricio Aylwin, remembered something Salvador Allende had once said to him at one of their numerous meetings held for the purpose of trying to reach an understanding: "This flesh is made of marble, senator," and he beat his thigh several times.

Senator Aylwin felt that Allende's suicide could be explained by the frivolous and self-aggrandizing course on which the president had embarked.

The suicide of Allende, affirmed Radomiro Tomic, candidate for the presidency of the republic in the elections won by Allende and founding member of the Christian Democratic Party, "does not mark the first chapter of a new era for Chile, but the last chapter of an old era."

Tomic, who from his home had followed the tragedy at the Moneda step by step, could not resign himself to the fact that its defenders had surrendered after only a few hours of struggle. While he was listening to the radio, he was reminded of the battle for Stalingrad, when the German army had to conquer the city stone by stone, room by room, since the rubble left by the shellings served as an ideal defense for the Soviet snipers. What would have happened if Allende had been sufficiently prepared to resist twenty-four hours instead of six? How would the rest of the world have reacted, such as the Security Council of the United Nations, for example? And what would the Chilean people, seeing a government fighting and not falling, have done?

Tomic concluded, "You can't have a revolution without revolutionaries."

But the ex-candidate was speaking *before* the Hawker Hunters proved the Moneda could be shelled without reducing the surrounding area to defensible rubble.

The archbishop of Santiago and head of the Chilean Catholic Church, Cardinal Raul Silva Henriquez, when he heard of the president's death, slowly shook his head.

"And I warned Allende so many times! Be careful about arming the paramilitary. They can't hold up against the armed forces."

The cardinal added, gravely shaking his head again, "It was useless. He would not understand, or they would not let him understand. I was present when, in my own house, Patricio Aylwin asked Allende to take immediate steps against the arming of the paramilitary forces. Allende seemed to be deaf, and of course he took no steps. He would have done something about it, but his own party prevented him."

For Hugo Vigorena, Chilean ambassador to Mexico during the Popular Unity government, the basic question is, that "we not kill Allende twice by again delaying the revolutionary process by our own divisions. If there was death at the Moneda, it was because the process was valid. And it will continue to be valid."

"Unlike a lot of people," said Mario Arnello, National Party deputy, "I was certain that Allende would try to achieve revolutionary success for his government, by any means whatsoever. If this didn't work out he'd try for a grand finale.

"I never thought that Allende, despite his frivolous life style, would agree to make an undramatic exit. His ambition to play a historic role was too strong.

"On one occasion, when he was talking to me, he told me frankly, 'Look, my friend, I have an historic vocation, and all that I have done and shall continue to do is in order to fulfill it.'

"We should remember that, in his first address as president of the republic, Allende compared the changes that his government would bring about with the experiments of Lenin.

"Lenin had created the dictatorship of the proletariat as a system for building socialism, he said. But, he, Allende, would build socialism through other means.

"Allende was a man always looking for ways to satisfy his tremendous ego. This ego influenced him even at the time of his death. He was well aware of the fact that he lived in a glass house and that it would be easy to destroy his image, for he led not a double, but a triple or quadruple life, and his handling of the public funds was open to question.

"During the final period of his life, and not merely during the last few minutes, he let himself be carried by the tide of events, unable to reason. Nor did he reason before he died, for he intended to surrender, but, at the end, when he was going to do so, he hesitated, returned, locked the door behind him, and killed himself. Some say that he even asked the doctor to pull the trigger.

"For the doctor, later, claimed that the reason why Allende

was not holding the machine gun in the proper position for shooting himself, was that he, the doctor, had removed it from him in order to ascertain whether he was still alive.

"But when half one's head has been blown off, it shouldn't be necessary for a doctor to remove the machine gun in order to see whether the victim is still alive!

"As for the claim that Allende was fighting at the time of his death, this is not certain either. Allende was sitting on a sofa, and this is a fact, for both the sofa and the curtain behind him were spattered with parts of the encephalic mass that had exploded in an upward direction.

"The story of Allende dying in combat is a fabrication by Fidel Castro, who also invented the story that Allende had wiped out an entire tank. . . ."

Allende and the Military

The scene of battle for General Augusto Pinochet Ugarte (the leader of the junta) was in an ancient and quiet residential sector of Santiago, situated in the first foothills of the Andes range, called Penalolen.

The eleventh day of September is over. Why was it staged?

"Because the armed forces could not remain indifferent to the chaos into which the government was dragging the nation. This is what led the commanders in chief to take over the control of the country."

"Any regrets?"

"I wish to point out that the members of the armed forces who have reached the apex of their careers prefer to stay at home. . . ."

"Satisfied?"

"The eleventh was carried out according to plan and was well coordinated."

"And the death of Allende?"

"Allende was asked on four occasions to hand over control. Faced with his refusal and the large amount of war materiel in the Moneda Palace, an attack was launched on the palace."

"How did he die?"

"Killed by a submachine gun given him by Fidel Castro."

"How was the coup kept secret?"

"Only a few officers were aware of what we were going to do. I sent them to Antofagasta, Iquique, Concepción, and Valdivia with the latest details in order to avoid unnecessary deaths. Everything worked out precisely because we employed an elemental principle of strategy. We made Mr. Allende worried about Valparaíso, when the hot spot was in Santiago."

"How were you appointed president of the junta?"

"For a while, it was actually a gentlemen's agreement. I don't expect to head the junta throughout its lifetime. We will rotate. Now I am president. Some time in the future it will be Admiral Merino, then General Leigh, and afterward General Mendoza. I have no interest in making myself irreplaceable. I have no aspiration other than to serve my country."

"And now?"

"We end the process and begin to build."

"How?"

"By bringing the country back to normal."

"Will it be easy?"

"All the provinces are under control."

"Any plan?"

"The second phase of economic reconstruction. A national balance sheet has been ordered to show the chaotic state the nation finds itself in."

"And after that?"

"As soon as the country has recuperated, the junta will hand the government over to whomever the people desire."

"What type of government will the junta exercise?"

"This is a national Chilean movement with no parallel to any other. The junta is not going to follow anybody else's pattern. We are a people that has lived under a democracy. There are no friends and foes here. Here there are just Chileans who must join together. We must all join together to work for the reconstruction of Chile."

"Was there any intervention from the United States in this uprising?"

"Not even my wife knew what was going on. Neither the United States nor any other country had anything to do with it."

"How long had you been waiting?"

"Since January we had been hoping for a dialogue between the Christian Democratic Party and the government. Allende deceived us. He made it clear that he was the principal opponent in a civil war, and our secret service had obtained photographs of the arsenal in the Moneda and in Tomas Moro."

"And the Chilean Marxists?"

"The Marxist parties must be outlawed because of their system, their personal morals, and their lack of ethics."

"General Gustavo Leigh, commander in chief of the Chilean air force, are you the harshest member of the military junta government?"

"I don't believe I am the harshest. Quite the contrary. My fame as a harsh man may be due to the way I emphasize everything I say, because I truly feel it. Certainly, we soldiers must be somewhat harsh because our profession is a harsh one and we see ourselves identified with this style of living, but in actual fact it cannot reveal what we truly feel inside."

"About the Popular Unity. . . ?"

"The people have been manipulated and deceived by the Popular Unity. One need only see how the leaders were living. They were sacred cows who claimed to be leading the 'people' to liberation. They have left the country in ruins, while they were living like maharajahs, indulging in whiskey, luxuries, minks, women, and delicacies. They thought that all they had to do to put themselves on a par with a worker was to appear in an open-necked shirt. They were hypocrites who were looting the country."

"And the country . . . what now?"

"I hope that the country will understand the reality it will have to live through after a three-year war that almost brought about its destruction. The junta cannot work miracles, but it is honest, truthful, and willing to work hard to put the country back on its feet. We are calling for work, work, and more work, in order to make a new nation of Chile."

"The most important challenge?"

"What I had to live through, six months before September 11, when we realized that Mr. Allende was incapable of saving the country from falling into an abyss and when we realized that part of his plan included the total collapse of Chile and the mass assassination of the high command of the armed forces and the carabineros in order to set up, right afterward, a problem-free government.

"This sinister Z Plan was thought out by President Allende's advisor, the Spaniard Joan Garces. This was a challenge to me and to all of us. [Even after a year of junta rule, the Z plan has not been persuasively documented. *Ed.*]

"We were confronted with a lying, deceitful, fawning government which used its 'political prowess' to divide and conquer. There came a moment when all we had to do was look each other in the eye to understand what the other was thinking. We did not need to hatch plots at secret meetings. Even the most humble soldier would ask us how long we were going to stand for it.

"Forty-eight hours before the eleventh, General Pinochet called me and said, 'Gustavo, you are not alone, the navy is not alone, nor will the army hold back, for none of us can tolerate any more of this.'

"And so an electrifying cohesion occurred between Admiral Merino, General Pinochet, and me.

"The following day we contacted the carabineros, who immediately informed us that they too were unwilling to tolerate any longer the situation in which the country now found itself. We all joined forces, each one assuming his own responsibility."

"The future?"

"We will all tighten out belts. We will not issue any more money, unlike Mr. Allende who issued twenty-seven times more currency than that circulating in the country during 1970."

"Commander in chief of the navy, Admiral José Toribio Merino, what about the eleventh?"

"The navy, which normally stays aloof from such commotion, could not remain indifferent to the national task. And this is why, without searching for any glory or power, we stepped in to help direct our country's destiny. For the armed institutions can serve no function if there is no fatherland."

"The Popular Unity?"

"The entire nation formed one state. This state, consisting of three powers, was crumbling. The executive power was forgetting its duty."

"Any regrets?"

"Our responsibility as Chileans and our pledge of honor led us to take on this responsibility which we did not seek. And although it is sad that a democratic tradition that for this continent was a long one has been broken, we found ourselves obliged to assume our responsibilities and, by mandate, assure the integrity of a state that had lost its inherent qualities."

"And Chile?"

"We are sure that the whole of Chile must understand the sacrifice that all of this represents. It must understand that for us, the navy, it is far easier and much more pleasant to remain at sea, stationed on our ships. But when there is a big job to be done, pleasant desires are forgotten, hearts unite, and institutions unite, for the fatherland stands above the wishes of each individual and it is to that fatherland that we dedicate all our efforts, no matter what the cost, no matter what the sacrifice."

"General director of the carabineros, Cesar Mendoza, why did you have the Carabineros Corps of Chile join the junta?"

"Because it was necessary to restore law and order, which had been seriously undermined. It has nothing to do with implanting ideological preferences or carrying out personal vendettas, but restoring public order and bringing the country back on the path of fulfillment of the constitution and laws of the republic. The spirit of the junta is to return to true lawfulness."

"The eleventh?"

"The eleventh was my birthday. . . . I got up a quarter to six in the morning. . . ."

"When did you know that the armed forces would stage an uprising?"

"At four o'clock in the afternoon of the tenth."

"And the Popular Unity?"

"For three years we were obeying delinquents. We carabineros have always been the 'vicars' of the armed forces. We obey without question."

"The future?"

"For the time being, we can't even blink! We are still in the first round of the fight. The Popular Unity organizations are still up and about. We still haven't found even half their armaments."

Vice-Admiral Carvajal, the chief of staff of the armed forces, was convinced that the bombing of the Moneda was a "punishment" to "cleanse" the palace of the iniquities that had sullied it and the name of Chile. For him, these flames symbolized the power and decisiveness of the armed forces. The bombing of the Moneda would serve as a warning to those who might resist the junta; in that sense, the speed and precision of the operation would save lives by discouraging further resistance.

On the other hand, La Moneda in flames was a finale that could have been avoided by Allende had he accepted the junta's terms. In any case, what had been inevitable for some time, in Carvajal's opinion, was the fall of the Popular Unity government.

"Allende did make some efforts to avoid it by—at a critical moment [October 1972]—bringing the armed forces into his cabinet.

"But those ministers of the armed branches of government," Vice-Admiral Carvajal mused in his fifth floor office, "received absolutely no support from the president. They were no more than figureheads, used to fool the country into thinking that the military were endorsing the program of the Popular Unity.

"So we decided that if the government wished a new military cabinet, it should not be like the previous one, when General Carlos Prats would issue an order, only to have it completely disregarded at the local level. A new military cabinet should contain a larger number of military ministers able to carry out a new government program, since the present one was leading the country to its destruction. Such a program would also require intermediary authorities to assure that the orders issued by the ministers would meet with true compliance. All these conditions were contained in a memorandum which was delivered to the commanders in chief, who were advised to follow them in the event that the president should decide to appoint more military ministers. In our opinion, there was no other way of achieving any success.

"However, despite these recommendations, Allende managed to appoint a cabinet composed of the three commanders in chief without intermediary supportive powers, and in complete disregard of these recommendations.

"With the exception of General Ruiz who had an understanding with his officers and could count on their loyalty, I believe that the other two commanders in chief were under the diabolical influence of that demon. They were hypnotized by him.

"Although it might seem ingenuous, they believed that a solution could be found by democratic means, if an understanding could be reached with the Christian Democrats, but even in those early days we had come to realize that words would get us nowhere.

"It was impossible to continue discussions, for we were acting in good faith and the government was acting in bad faith, with constant lies. That is what brought us to the conclusion that some action had to be taken, for words were useless.

"But action was being obstructed by those commanders in chief under the influence of the devil. They would not speak out or take any action. Then the events were unleashed which, within a few days, brought about the resignation of the commanders in chief, not only from their offices as such, but also from their respective ministries.

"This also led to the abandonment of the idea that it was possible to continue conversations and discussions. The same thing happened during the days of our independence when everyone came to realize that they could not continue to depend on the king of Spain.

"Action had to be taken, which soon received the support of all the citizens, the unions, the women, Congress, the Supreme

Court, the Treasury, and this support strengthened our conviction more and more that this was an illegitimate government acting against the wishes of the large majority of the country.

"This pressure from the citizenry was never exerted through any political party, with which I have never been associated, but rather it was a direct pressure from the population.

"We prepared our plan to silence the telecommunications well in advance. We were counting on two important factors in order to assure our success: first, the Arms Control Law [which authorizes the armed forces to search private property without warning for hidden arms] enabled us to take preventive measures. Second, the State Internal Security Law, which, in the plan we had developed, would allow us to handle strike situations that might arise in various public utilities.

"With the telecommunications and the public utilities under our protection, it was very easy to act, because basically, half the country thereby fell under our control. The assault on the Moneda had not been included in the State Internal Security plans, but it was relatively simple to work out.

"Only the high command of the four branches of the armed forces participated in the early meetings. Then a trusted group of their respective staff drew up, in greater detail, the corresponding plans. Since the plan was based on provisions of the Arms Control Law and the State Internal Security Law, the structure for action was already in place. All we had to do was use these provisions aggressively.

"We had to act quickly because of the possibility of extremist forces, with or without the government's consent, staging a countercoup of their own. For instance, here, in this very office, Clodomiro Almeyda, who at that time was defense minister, after being told how upset we were by the general violence, lawbreaking, indiscriminate seizures of companies, and the formation of armed industrial cordons [organizations linking all factories within an area to coordinate the workers' resistance to a rightist-military coup], confessed to us that those cordons no longer fell within the framework of governmental organizations, that they had already exceeded the government's line of action, and that attempts were being made, by persuasion only, to convince them to return the companies that had been illegally seized and the arms that were in their possession.

"It was therefore logical for us to think that the moment might come when these cordons would attack the government, maintaining that it was too weak, or objecting to its contracts with the Christian Democrats, or claiming that it was a reformist government that had betrayed the revolution.

"Consequently, we also put together a plan to come to the defense of the government, in the event of an attack from the industrial cordons.

"To all this must be added the declaration made to us by Allende himself at a meeting of the Higher Council for National Defense. Taking his leave of all the councilors, he concluded the session with the words, 'This is perhaps the last time we shall meet, for the danger of civil war is imminent.'

"I called together that same day the other staff officers and said to them, 'We find ourselves faced with two facts. First, Minister Almeyda has said that the industrial cordons have overstepped the government's guidelines. Second, the president told us today that civil war is imminent.' This took place on August 22, 1973. From that moment on it was our duty to prepare ourselves in order to prevent this war.

"Now comes the second part, the rebuilding of the country."

Allende and the
Christian Democratic Party

Eduardo Novoa, one of the most important figures in Allende's government at the start of the presidency, set himself the task of examining all legal provisions existing to date that would allow the program of the Popular Unity to be put into effect.

During the final weeks preceding the fall of Allende's regime, Novoa was in Paris, heading a Chilean group which was trying to override the blockades organized against Chilean copper by North American companies whose assets in Chile had been nationalized. Novoa's group was also attempting to renegotiate loans from various international credit agencies which had been influenced by the nationalized copper companies to withhold them from the Allende government.

But on the day of the military uprising, Eduardo Novoa and his wife had just arrived in Salonika for a vacation, and the fulfillment of an old dream, to make a tour of Greece.

Novoa, who spoke no Greek, was listening to the radio in his car and heard the name of Chile repeated several times and saw it written in large letters in the newspaper headlines. When he was finally able to understand what had happened, he returned to Paris in three days, retracing a route that, on his way out, had taken him six days. In Novoa's view, written in Mexico after the coup, the villain of the piece was the Christian Democratic Party:

"The results of the presidential election of September 4, 1970, are public knowledge. None of the three candidates obtained an absolute majority. Allende won with a little under thirty-seven percent of the votes, and Tomic suffered a bitter defeat.

"The Plenary Congress, made up of both Senate and House, chose the president from the two leading candidates, Allende and Alessandri. The Christian Democrats agreed to vote for Allende only after they obtained his agreement to a constitutional reform the avowed object of which was to assure respect for constitutional freedoms, but which in fact represented the government's submission, right from the start, to restrictions and limitations previously unknown by any other Chilean president. A left-winger could not step into the presidency with all the attributes and juridical powers with which his predecessors—even the right-wing extremists!—had governed! His wings had to be clipped right from the beginning!

"In Chile, it had been customary for some time for presidential platforms to be nothing more than a means to capture votes. Once in power, the elected soon forgot them. This was not true of Allende, however. He could not hope for any help from new laws passed by a Congress whose majority were opposed to him—the only exception being the complete nationalization of copper, unanimously approved thanks to strong pressure from public opinion. Instead, government began the difficult task of drawing up a list of even the most ancient laws, many long since forgotten, that would enable the Popular Unity program to be carried out.

"Despite the intricate restrictions, cleverly woven to deprive him of legislative leverage, and the national custom of forgetting campaign promises, Allende maintained his firm intention to transform the basic structures of Chile and provoked the wrath and envy of the Christian Democratic Party. For if this transformation was achieved, the chances for men of his stamp in future elections could then be assured.

"So an all-out effort was launched to suppress even these ancient laws which might allow President Allende to follow through on the promises made to the people by the Popular Unity.

"The Christian Democratic Party tried to maintain the *appearance* of a democratic operation, but in actual fact, it was doing everything possible to manacle the executive power and to prevent it from governing. Its congressional opposition was tenacious and merciless, and by this means it was able to unseat various ministers of state, by accusing them of legal violations of which they were innocent.

"The policy of the opposition, formed by the closely united Christian Democrats and right-wingers, resorted to extreme measures of encirclement and obstructionism in order to undermine the government. It was based on the hope that the moment would come when Allende, totally impeded in his actions, would resign from office, but its supporters were unaware of Allende's fortitude and determination. Events soon showed that Allende would not abandon voluntarily the high office he had been legally placed in by the people's mandate.

"From that point on, the declared purpose of the Right and of the majority of the Christian Democrats was to prepare the climate conducive to a military uprising.

"The declaration in the House that President Allende had violated the constitution and its laws and had lost his legitimacy was, besides being false, an open invitation to the armed forces to bring about the coup. This declaration could have been made in legitimate form within a special process provided for in the constitution, but this would have required for approval a two-thirds majority of the congressional votes.

"Having been made outside any such procedural process and without the required majority, it was perforce an act juridically vitiated (since no public organ is empowered, within a state de jure, with any attributes other than those expressly and specifically conferred upon it by law), and with no legal effect whatsoever.

"But the intent was that the military consider itself morally freed from its pledge of loyalty to the chief of state.

"Direct words of encouragement to the military chiefs to abandon their obligation of obedience issued also from the mouths of highly placed Christian Democrats. Meanwhile, the CIA, the extreme right wing, and the international companies added their support to this crafty maneuver and exacerbated the economic chaos that was gripping the country.

"When Cardinal Silva, discerning the tragic end to which these tactics were leading, wanted to bring about an entente between the Popular Unity and the Christian Democrats, the latter did not wish to draw back from their antidemocratic design. The Christian Democrats, as a ploy to break up the discussions, demanded that the Popular Unity, which was the legitimate government, agree to carry out a Christian Democratic platform, as if, in a democracy, it were the vanquished who were entitled to impose its criteria on the victors, namely the government.

"All that the Christian Democratic Party needed to do in order to avert a military uprising was to allow the Popular Unity government to follow through on a minimum portion of its program. Nevertheless, the party chose to push matters to their farthest limits in order to bring about the coup they so fervently desired.

"Direct responsibility falls, of course, on the leader, Frei, and Party President Aylwin, who gave their explicit approval to the military coup after its occurrence, and also on the majority of the militants who lent their support.

"But many more enlightened leaders who now deeply regret the military dictatorship must also accept a clear share of the blame through their inaction.

"Ex-candidate Tomic, giving in to a passionate and extremely personal reaction, did not attempt to offer any guidance to his party.

"Leighton, the old figurehead. who offered 'even to make friends with the devil' in order to preserve liberties which were never threatened by the Popular Unity, must now start looking for who knows what sort of friend.

"Fuentealba, ex-party leader [before Patricio Aylwin], who warned of the danger at the eleventh hour, was the originator and driving force behind one of the political ploys which shrewdly took advantage of the opposition in order to bring about the overthrow of Allende.

"All of these now deplore the bloody repressions and confiscation of liberties. Nevertheless, their tears must now be stinging also from the saltiness of remorse for what they did not do, but could have."

"You can't hold conversations with a cocked pistol," said Patricio Alywin, senator and leader of the Christian Democratic Party. "I cannot sit down and negotiate with someone who receives me with a machine gun on the table.

"Yet this was what was happening in Chile, because officially, through repeated exhortations by Popular Unity parties and sectors attached to the government that the so-called people's power be maintained, the actions of armed groups was fomented and stimulated, including the distribution of light and heavy arms of all calibers in the expectation that Chileans could be intimidated.

"As long as the government tolerated such a situation, it could not expect to hold a dialogue with us who bore no arms other than our reasoning and our democratic vocation to express our thinking and defend what we considered to be the true interests of Chile. The government bore the responsibility to create the basic conditions for a democratic dialogue if, in fact, it really did wish to save the constitution."

Cardinal Raul Henriquez commented:

"We have worked to bring about a dialogue between the Christian Democrats and the government at an extremely difficult time in the life of this country. We did not impose any condition as regards the form that the dialogue should take. Consequently, we cannot be held responsible for its outcome. All that we wished, during such a dark moment, was that the Church of Chile fulfill its mission as peacemaker."

Bernardo Leighton is a Christian Democratic deputy who was minister of the interior and vice-president of the republic during the goverment of Eduardo Frei.

"I have known Allende since 1931. I believe that he was a loyal democrat right from the beginning to the end of his government, and that he fought within the Popular Unity to impose this ideal. I believe that one need only reread the articles reported in the press of the left wing and far left wing during the last few years, to see and discover attacks against Salvador Allende, which clearly demonstrate that certain extremist sectors of the Popular Unity parties did not agree with the position taken by the president concerning problems requiring an urgent solution. And it was this disagreement that gave rise to the conversations between the Christian Democrats and President Allende. On many questions they came very close to reaching a solution, and in others, concrete solutions were in fact reached.

"In my opinion, the possibility of reaching a concrete consensus on formulas that could be followed to resolve the difficulties remained always open and viable. That is why I have never tried to justify the military rebellion by claiming, as many have done, that it has its raison d'être in the stalemate that had developed with regard to the search for solutions to the problems besetting the country.

"As far as the Popular Unity is concerned, I believe that by overriding and opposing the line Allende wished to follow with his government, the coalition made his policies appear to be born of a form of sectarian dogmatism that was very detrimental to the democratic transformation of the country."

Bernardo Leighton; Ignacio Palma, ex-president of the Senate; Renan Fuentealba, senator and ex-Chilean delegate to the United Nations; Radomiro Tomic, ex-candidate for the presidency of the republic and ex-Chilean ambassador to the United States; Fernando Sanhueza, ex-president of the Chamber of Deputies; Sergio Saavedra, ex-governor of Santiago; Claudio Huepe, deputy; Andrews Aylwin, deputy; Mariano Ruiz-Esquide, deputy; Waldemar Carrasco, deputy; Jorge Cash, professor and journalist; Jorge Donoso, attorney; Belisario Velasco, economist; Ignacio Balbontin, sociologist; and Florencio Ceballos, attorney, signed the following political declaration:

On this day, September 13, 1973, the undersigned, in witness of the fact that this is the first occasion on which we are able to meet for the purpose of discussing our mutual views and explaining our political position, following the military coup of the day before yesterday, do hereby declare the following:

1. We categorically condemn the overthrow of the constitutional president of Chile, Mr. Salvador Allende, whose government—by virtue of the wish of the people and the decision of our party—we invariably opposed. We pay respectful

homage to the sacrifice he made by giving his life in the defense of his constitutional authority.

2. We wish to point out that our opposition to his government was always aimed at preserving the continuity of the process of change which the Christian Democratic government had the honor of initiating in our country, and, at the same time, at preventing its deviation on to an antidemocratic path.

We maintain in all its aspects the criticism we leveled at the government of the Popular Unity and of President Allende in this regard. We therefore reiterate that, in conformity with the Christian Democratic ethic, we never held any other parliamentary or individual posture that did not constitute opposition within the democratic ethic, aimed at rectifying the errors committed by President Allende's government and impugned by us.

3. The lack of any rectification of these errors, which finally led us to this tragedy, is the responsibility of all of us, government and opposition, for no one can evade his duty to uphold the democracy.

However, in our judgment, there were those who bear the greater share of the responsibility in this tragedy: in the first place, the sectarian dogmatism of the Popular Unity coalition, unable to build a truly democratic way toward socialism, suited to our own particular way of life; the irresponsibility of the Far Left merits particular censure.

In the second place, the economic right wing which, with cold calculation, approved the errors committed by the Popular Unity in order to create a climate of tension, obfuscation, and political extremism which, together with the above, rendered even a minimal consensus impossible for those of us who were striving to reach it with objectivity and judiciousness.

4. These extremist groups recruited public opinion and even numerous political and military leaders, creating the false impression that there was no way out of the Chilean crisis other than an armed confrontation and a military coup.

We reiterate today, as before, our deep conviction that we

could have avoided in Chile the implantation of a totalitarian regime, within the confines of the democratic ethic, and without the unnecessary cost in lives and excesses inherent in any solution imposed by force.

5. The military junta has expressed its intention to restore power to the will of the people and to respect public freedoms. We welcome this intention as a positive one, conducive to the restoration of democracy and peace in our society, and we hope that this intention will be fulfilled without delay, in accordance with the statements made.

6. As far as we are concerned, we consider that our greatest duty at this time, one that we assume above all others, is to pursue our struggle to uphold the principles of the Christian Democratic Party, and to restore democracy in Chile, without which those principles have no meaning.

The events which today we deplore prove that only through liberty, enjoyed by the majority of the people and not by an exclusive minority, can we aspire to the humanistic and democratic transformation of Chile, which constitutes our aim and strengthens our will.

Allende and the Unions

Leon Vilarin is the president of the Confederation of Truck Owners. Vilarin owns a truck. In Chile there are 47,200 trucks distributed among almost as many different owners. If a truck comes to a standstill through lack of spare parts, then the trucker's life and the life of his family come to a standstill too. Spare parts began to be in short supply during Allende's presidency because there wasn't any foreign currency to import them. The truckers protested to the government.

The government wanted to create a state trucking industry, and the truckers felt their very survival threatened and made further demands upon the government.

The truckers would not give in, the government would not give in. The truckers realized that their strength was in their unity, and they united the 135 different syndicates existing in the country under one single management, a union. It was an effective union, able to face up to the government without the mediation of any political party.

"Chile, a party-conscious country since the beginning of its history, looked on in amazement at this new force of unionization. The response was not long in coming!

"Professionals unionized, merchants unionized, wives, students, businessmen, bankers.

"The political parties also reacted by trying to capture this new force . . . but too late, they'd missed the boat! The die had been cast, the unions had already launched their attack against the government. Allende must either meet their demands or resign.

"The weapon of the unions was national stoppage.

"The government's reaction: this is a conspiracy hatched by North American imperialism and carried out by seditious extremists who want nothing more than to bring down the people's legitimate government. The armed forces, meanwhile, were watching both sides and drawing their own conclusions."

Leon Vilarin expressed his feelings about Allende's death: "I don't approve of suicide. He should have faced the judgment of the people, but he didn't dare."

Professionals in Chile, grouped under a multiunion leadership, had decreed on September 10 an indefinite nationwide stoppage until President Allende either made substantial improvements or resigned.

They gave as their reasons for this stoppage ever-increasing restrictions placed on private enterprise, undermining of expertise and efficiency by the ascendancy of an unrestrained proselytism, an inflammatory sectarian attitude transforming places of work into scenes of bitter power struggles, the collective pressure from groups, in many cases armed, that was superseding decisions that should be based on science and technology.

In addition, the professionals held the government responsible for the loss of respect for hierarchy, that business management had fallen into inefficient and irresponsible hands, and that there had been an exodus of professionals caused by these circumstances. Disregard on the part of the executive power in letter and spirit, of both the legal and constitutional order and of the hierarchical principles inherent in any sound administration was also blamed on Allende's government.

Allende and the Parties: From Far Right to Far Left

Pablo Rodriguez Grez is the leader of "Patria y Libertad" ("Fatherland and Freedom"). This movement was born on September 13, 1970, "with the sole purpose of assuring that Salvador Allende would not be elected president," according to the words of Rodriguez himself.

Briefly, the plan was that the legislature proclaim Jorge Alessandri the winner, and that Alessandri then resign, thus necessitating new elections, but this time with the Christian Democrats and the National Party, both being represented by one single candidate, assuring for themselves jointly more than sixty percent of the votes. With Allende's victory, Patria y Libertad decided to take clandestine armed action.

"Many will think that force cannot be used as an instrument of political action to abolish force," explains Rodriguez.

"Those who pass these judgments upon us have never known or lived through what we have lived through. The traditional game of politics lacks effectiveness and relevance in the fight against international Marxist-Leninism.

"These people extol the classic values—liberty, the fatherland, the de jure state, lawfulness—as long as these values serve their purposes, but they become implacable to the point of mocking these values and trampling on them if they come in the way of their goals.

"This was the invariable trend in Chile for three years. Neither the democratic dialogue, nor the plight of the people, nor the brotherhood born of a common historic destiny would make them retrace a single step, unless for the strategic purpose of thereby advancing two steps forward, in accordance with Lenin's teachings.

"The international Communist movement, supported by the socialist nations throughout the world and endowed with money for propaganda, infiltration, and political action running into the multimillions, must be eradicated by force, for it proclaims force and the revolutionary ethic as the most expeditious and effective means of seizing power.

"This is why we believe that those who fight international Marxist-Leninism with the traditional tools of bourgeois and liberal democracy are simply opening the doors to a Marxist-Leninist takeover."

Patria y Libertad made every effort within its power to bring about, with or without arms, the fall of the Popular Unity government. As a result of his commitments to the unsuccessful subversive plans of the Second Tank Regiment under Lieutenant Colonel Roberto Souper Onfray on June 29, 1973, Pablo Rodriguez sought asylum in the Ecuadorian Embassy. He then managed to reach Ecuador and secretly entered Chile through Argentina by the Maulin Malal Cordilleran pass, about 440 miles south of Santiago, in the early days of September.

"On the night of the tenth, Rodriguez took a sleeping pill, gave orders not to be awoken the next morning, and fell asleep, already knowing what would happen the next day, for he said, 'Let whatever must happen, happen. I don't believe in anything anymore.' "

"Allende's suicide," Rodriguez declared six weeks after the coup, "can be looked at from two points of view. In the first place, I was deeply impressed with Allende's tremendous loyalty to international Marxism. I believe that Allende was more international-Marxist than Chilean. He realized that he was going to be far less useful alive than dead. In the second place, I believe he did not have sufficient courage to face the judgment of a people that was going to become deeply aware of what was happening in Chile."

"The Communist Party is mostly to blame for the death of Allende and the fall of the people's government."

This assertion was made by a young member of the Movement of the Revolutionary Left (MIR), hiding in a residential section of Santiago and forced to move from one address to another continually.

"The Communist Party did whatever it could to prevent, firstly, that the people be armed and, secondly, that the people be able to count on loyalty from the armed forces.

"Not only did the Communist Party give us no support, but it even attacked us because we were calling on the soldiers, the sailors, the airmen, the carabineros, to disobey the orders from their command to stage a coup, and to defend the workers and not the bosses.

"Communist Senator Volodia Teitelboim accused us of being hotheaded, of scaring the middle class and playing into the hands of the fascists.

"The Communist Party allowed and supported the entry into

the government of the subversive high command of the armed forces; it permitted and supported a reformism the obvious result of which was loss of power for the people and the recovery of power for the bosses.

"If, in three years, we were able to create armed forces that were capable of defending the people, its government, and its president, we owe this mostly to the Communist Party. I hope that by this time they have learned their lesson."

Sergio Diez, a senator of the National Party, summed up Allende's presidency:

"The law of the jungle held sway over the country during the government of the Popular Unity: in industry, in commerce, in the fields. More than 1,500 small agricultural landowners turned to me for help. It was always the same: two members of the Movement of the Revolutionary Left arrived on the scene and sided with two workers. They took advantage of the very first time the landlord was away to 'seize' the land.

"Upon his return, the landowner forbade them to enter his house, went to the carabineros, and denounced them for usurpation, but the carabineros had orders from the Ministry of the Interior not to intervene.

"Then the landowner turned to a lawyer in order to bring suit for illegal seizure. At best, the judge would order the expulsion of the 'occupants' and ask the governor for police intervention to see that the ruling was duly executed.

"The governor, an appointee of the Popular Unity, would not allow the police's intervention, and the landlord then appealed to the courts. The court issued a complaint to the president, and the president notified the governor, who in turn appointed a mediator.

"By this time, the small landowner, unable to work since he

was denied access to his own property, without money, and totally demoralized, pleaded to the Agrarian Reform Corporation to expropriate his land at any price.

"This lack of judicial defense gave the farmers the right to rebel; they unionized and initiated a movement to recover their property by force. It was the law of the jungle."

"And the eleventh?"

"That day I was playing a game of golf."

Carlos Briones had been convinced for some time that the Popular Unity would meet a sorry end if it did not change its precipitous course.

"The events have confirmed my fears," he had said, "Allende's three years of government drastically changed the country's infrastructure, economy. system of land ownership. banking. . . .

"But the process had to be arrested in order to organize it into an ordered and judicial structure, for I am basically a jurist, and I believe in the law.

"It had become essential to rectify the situation and, most of all, to waste no time in reestablishing the social discipline that had become severely undermined by the influence exerted by groups who were more dedicated to political activism than increasing national production and making sure the process would be an orderly one.

"The vertical structure of power or 'law and order,' had to be reestablished as well, so that the ministers could make decisions which were implemented without being permanently obstructed by politically inspired decisions from the parties.

"President Allende, I believe, shared my view, and I don't see why I should think otherwise, despite other people's beliefs that it was not so and that the president was simply treading water to gain time and appease certain sectors, especially the armed forces.

"On the other hand, Senator Altamirano's observations and statements were quite different from my own, throughout the period of Allende's presidency.

"I was in the center of a struggle that developed between the president's positions and those of the Socialist Party because the policy I was trying to carry out was not only mine but also Allende's. By attacking me, the Socialist Party was also attacking the president. It was an absurd, paradoxical situation. One lived in an incredible climate of political irrationality: a theater of the absurd that outdid Beckett."

El Siglo (The Century), the official newspaper of the Chilean Communist Party, expressed the party's attitude to the armed forces only three days before the coup:

> The right-wingers have for some time been carrying out a deliberate and foolhardy attempt to bring about a coup, by various actions: terrorist, political, or outright seditious strikes against businesses.
>
> Brazenly, they even call publicly for the overthrow of the constitutional government. They want to make people believe that the interests of the armed forces are contrary to the interests of the entire people and of the legitimate government. The contradictions that exist are between the people and the oligarchy, imperialism and those who violate the law and who pretend to be unaware of the will of the citizenry by trying to bring about a coup d'état.
>
> They accuse the government of having acted illegally, of being illegitimate, but it is they who advocate, organize, and promote the most brutal of all violations: civil war and a coup d'état.
>
> Unable now to hold back the tide of history and the will of the people, they want to provoke a violent, criminal revolt against democracy. They are desperately trying to carry out their

anticonstitutional plans. They want to recover the power they had lost, by spilling the blood of the workers, of the people.

The Rightists, the high conspiratorial command, are desperate. They realize that the government's measures have managed to assure a substantial improvement in the conditions of the people over the next several months and better days appear on the horizon for the next year. This is why their craze for a coup is becoming more obvious with each passing day. This is why they are now looking for any pretext whatsoever, use any infamy whatsoever, in order to deal a blow to the fatherland.

But this is wishful thinking. They forget that the armed forces adhere to their institutional doctrine with respect to the constitution and the laws; they don't want to understand that the armed forces are not guardians of special economic or financial interests, but guardians of the fatherland, of national sovereignty, of national security.

But above all, they forget that Chile has a people, a working class, whose breast and heart are the cuirass that shall defend the government—the people's government—right to the bitter end.

Allende and the Workers

November 10, 1973. The town of La Legua is one of many which make up the industrial belt of Santiago. About 15,000 people live there: sixty percent are industrial workers, thirty percent are businessmen, and ten percent are unemployed. They live in one-story houses, some painted green, others pink. They call them "emergency houses." The atmosphere is peaceful. There is a small Catholic church, Our Lady of Peace, and children play in the streets.

"What happened in La Legua on the eleventh?"

"There was a lot of shooting," said one of the town's leaders, "a lot of shooting. Carabineros and townspeople died. About thirty carabineros died, but not here in La Legua. Only a few died here, about sixteen civilians, but everything was blamed on La Legua because there are a lot of unemployed people here.

"But now there aren't any. They have all gone away, or been killed.

"There were about eighty people here fighting the carabineros.

"They brought us weapons from outside. Everything was here: machine guns, pistols, rifles, everything. We didn't know what party they belonged to—those guys who brought in the weapons—but they handed them over to us and taught us how to use them. Right here, on this corner, for example, there was a guy with a bazooka and another one throwing grenades."

"Is the fighting still going on?"

"No, but persecution is. A lot of it. They are persecuting the people who were the leaders of the Neighborhood Councils and on the Boards of Prices and Supplies.

"There was a leader of the Neighborhood Council who didn't belong to any party, and they took him away to an island.

"There is also persecution in the industries.

"I was one of those they fired.

"I used to work in the Andina Coca-Cola Bottling Factory, which was a state-controlled industry and belonged to the semipublic ownership category, and since I was only a seasonal worker, they threw me out. There were seventy of us who were let go.

"A colonel arrived, who had been appointed state inspector, and he threw out all the seasonal workers. They only gave us seventy escudos each, which can't even pay for our cigarettes.

"Now I have to spend my time selling poultry and eggs. There's enough to live on. All of us who have been let go, we get along by helping each other. They say that we are criminals, but all we want is a chance. We're all equal human beings. I've never stuck my nose into politics. Soccer, that's another matter, but politics—never!"

"The Popular Unity?"

"Well, before [during Allende's presidency], you could afford yourself the luxury of buying a pair of shoes for three thousand escudos, but now no one can buy them. Before, we used to buy leather shoes for the kids, but now we can only buy them plastic shoes. It's true that before, we had a queue up for everything, but there was money around. I prefer to stand in line with money in my pocket than not to stand in line and walk around with my pockets empty! Don't you agree?"

"And you, senora?"

"They killed my husband. He'd gone to play a game of soccer with a few friends. They were at the home of one of the friends when the carabineros from the twelfth Commissariat arrived. It was about half past ten in the morning. They put them in the van and started to beat them up right there and then. They then took them to the twelfth Commissariat. I went to look for him, but they told me he was in the National Stadium [in Santiago]. He wasn't in the stadium either. I went back to the twelfth, and they told me that if my husband had anything on his record, I'd better not go on looking for him. And my husband did have a record. He was on file. I found him later in the Macul Department; he had fifteen bullets in his body.

"I also saw the dead bodies of the other friends.

"Afterward, I went to file a complaint with the Bureau of Investigation and spoke with the chief officer who took down my statement. He told me that the carabineros had orders not to kill anyone, but that they were doing it without authorization. Then the statement was passed on to the government junta, and that is why the killings here have stopped."

THE GONZALESES

A Chilean Dialogue

The Gonzales family is fictitious, yet in their passionate and confused arguments over what the events occurring in their country meant for them, they are representative of thousands of Chilean families.

Salvador Allende Gossens's great experiment, the creation of "A Chilean Road to Socialism," spoke directly to the individual citizen, provoking responses which ranged from sour resistance to wild enthusiasm. Allende, in his sister's words quoted earlier in this book, "demanded changes in the individual ... which often were not realized because external events occurred far more rapidly than the internal or personal ones."

The painful divisions within the Gonzaleses illuminate both the difficulty and the urgency of those individual transformations.

At 7:30 on the morning of the eleventh, the alarm rang at the home of the Gonzaleses, a small apartment on the fourth floor of a great block in a residential neighborhood of Santiago.

Elena was thirty-three years old with two children, seven and nine years old. She was a graduate of the National Teaching Institute, but was not teaching at the moment. Julian, thirty-nine years old, was head of a department in a Santiago bank and an expert in statistics.

Elena switched off the alarm and got out of bed. Still drugged with sleep, she went into the small modern kitchen, turned on the radio, put water in the kettle, and turned on the stove.

She soon realized that the radio was silent and thought it might be the batteries. She switched from one station to the next until she found one still broadcasting.

The navy had revolted, and Valparaíso had fallen. The people should take their battle positions.

She stifled a scream of excitement and ran back to the bedroom.

"Julian, Julian, wake up. The coup, we've had a coup. I swear it to you. Valparaíso has fallen. The navy has revolted."

Julian Gonzales looked at his wife angrily. "Anyone would think you're announcing the arrival of Santa Claus. So, those apes have finally made up their minds."

"I suppose you are happy," Julian said finally, in a weary voice.

"Yes," answered Elena.

"Happy," repeated Julian and, getting out of bed, went into the kitchen. "Happy because those apes have managed to get together to strangle one of the most venerable democratic traditions of the world. Happy because our noble and professional armed forces have finally decided to let down their masks to ally with the strong men with whom they have always been friendly anyway. Happy because the workers and the poor of this country have lost their only chance to govern themselves with dignity after having waited for this opportunity for nearly three hundred years."

This was too much for Elena.

"Happy because we have just eliminated the most incompetent, least Chilean, most corrupt, and most hypocritical government which this country has had in all of its history."

"Wait! The last word is still to be said," answered Julian, shaking with indignation. "There still might remain somewhere a handful of soldiers loyal to the constitution they have sworn to defend."

"The constitution that Allende made a mockery of anytime

he could," answered Elena trying hard to control her anger.

"Have you even been prevented from reading a paper dedicated to insulting the government?" asked Julian. "Or delighting in those TV programs slandering the entire Popular Unity coalition? You've been able to start your day listening to those morons insulting the people on all the opposition radios. Tell me, then, how has Allende made a mockery of the constitution? Did you even lose the right to parade in the streets? No, you did not! You exercised that right which the president respected by joining that shameful demonstration of the pots and pans where all the rich Santiago women complained because they could no longer live off the fat of the land. Have the police ever raided your home because you thought differently from the government? Have they?

"Let me tell you something. With this coup we have really lost our freedom. You will find out the hard way that the Popular Unity coalition respected you as they did everyone, equally, without restricting what you were thinking, or what you were saying, or what kind of friends you had, or how much money you had, or by what name you were called. Then you will regret saying that the Popular Unity made a mockery of the constitution!"

"All right. It didn't violate it because it couldn't," answered Elena. "But Mr. Novoa made a mockery of the constitution by handling it like an old prostitute, trying to squeeze out of her anything he could for the sake of Marxism. Mr. Allende made a mockery of it by surrounding himself with personal friends armed to the teeth. Mr. Altamirano made a mockery of it trying to incite the navy into an uprising against its own officers. Do you think the Chileans are such idiots that they can be fooled by having freedom of the press, while behind their backs the country was being ransacked and led toward Marxist dictatorship?"

"Marxist dictatorship!" sneered Julian. "Don't you think

that charge is rather too hackneyed to be taken seriously? Who can believe such nonsense when it has been used by all the fascist apes in the world."

"I believe in it," asserted Elena. "I am sure there is no Marxism that does not seek dictatorship, be it that of the proletariat or that of Fidel Castro. And Popular Unity is no exception.

"Our brave soldiers have been hearing our cries in these interminable three years during which we have lost everything, including our dignity. We have been misled by a vain hypocrite who claims to be helping the people while he lives like a king, with four homes, eating caviar and drinking whiskey, while the people struggle to buy a loaf of bread. We have had to put up with so many empty words, so much hypocrisy. We have seen how those people they call 'new men' live, they are 'new' because never before have we seen such shameless thievery. They insolently run around in their Fiat 125s, like feudal lords surveying their domain. I don't believe in democratic Marxists."

"Allende is one, and he has shown it."

"Allende can't even keep order in his own house," exclaimed Elena, "and everyone knows this except you and him."

The voice of Allende speaking over the radio interrupted her.

"I shall not give up. I call on the workers to remain at their stations in the factory or plants. I am at this moment anticipating expressions of support from soldiers determined to defend their government. I renew my determination to continue to defend Chile. I intend to resist with what I have, even at the cost of my life. . . ."

"And the lives of a million Chileans," said Elena, unable to contain herself.

Julian, deeply moved by the words of his president, seemed not to hear.

It was several hours later. The junta had declared its intention to bomb the Moneda at eleven—where Allende was making his last stand.

"They won't dare," Julian Gonzales said out loud, nervously pacing the narrow terrace of his apartment and scanning the gray sky.

"They won't get him out of the Moneda with bombs or anything else," remarked Elena. "He has been after the presidency for twenty years. He isn't about to leave now. I tell you bombs won't get him out, but if they don't get him out now he is going to make himself president for life."

"Don't talk nonsense!"

"Nonsense, is it nonsense to think that a Marxist doesn't care a rap for what they call 'a bourgeois constitution' and that the only thing he does care about is how to make fun of it so he can remain in power forever?"

"Allende has never tried to remain in power, and he has promised he would step down and give his post to whoever shall win the 1976 elections."

"Then as a Marxist Mr. Allende is a failure because he will have to hand over the government to Eduardo Frei. That's why I am amazed Mr. Allende has gotten this far: he is a lousy Marxist, a lousy doctor, a lousy economist, a lousy husband, a—"

"Shut up!" exclaimed Julian. "How dare you talk that way about a man who is offering his life at this moment to defend the laws, the justice and freedom of this country. If this man had not had the courage to face all alone the armed forces of the country, or if the people and their leaders do not help him right away, there will be nothing noble left in Chile—no elections, no parties, no Congress, no university, no press, no dignity, nothing."

"And what about food, and places to live, where are they? Construction is at a standstill. Children can go to school only three out of nine months. Half the professionals have already left the country, the other half are on strike. Those who are at the university spend all their time in political warfare. Prosperity, and order, and progress and utensils and buses and—and some peace at least in the families. Where are all these things?" Elena was shouting, and close to tears.

The bombs were dropped on the Moneda at eleven thirty.

"They are going to kill him," Julian Gonzales said sorrowfully. Looking toward the great column of smoke he was able to see from his terrace he added, "They are going to burn him alive."

"Why doesn't he surrender?" asked Elena. "Or does he still believe that the industrial cordons led by Mr. Altamirano are going to save him?"

Julian did not answer. He had to admit there was little time left, and the people had not come to the defense of their government. Deep down he shared his wife's dislike for Mr. Altamirano. He realized that it was Altamirano who was adding more fuel to the fire which was now burning the "Peaceful Road toward Socialism." Now when it was the conciliatory Allende who took up arms, it was Altamirano who was noticeable by his absence. At the hour of truth, when brave words must give way to brave deeds there was no Carlos Altamirano; there was no Miguel Enriquez, chief of the Movement of the Revolutionary Left; there was no Victor Toro, leader of the Revolutionary People's Front; there was no Oscar Guillermo Garreton, leader of the Movement of Unified Popular Action. Without their leaders, how could the workers rise up to defend their government?

These absent leaders were a source of grief for Julian Gonzales. He was unable to explain them to himself or to his wife. Sensing his confusion she blurted out,

"Popular Unity has been nothing more than a myth to gather

votes. During good times all they did was fight within each ministry for even the least important public post. During hard times their unity consists of screaming, 'Save yourself if you can.' Tell me the truth, Julian, where is the unity of the Popular Unity?"

Julian's reply was immediate. "In Allende," he shouted. "In Allende dead or alive!"

The junta's proclamation over, the radio had further divided the Gonzaleses.

"They are right," thought Elena Gonzales, listening to a broadcast which denounced the Popular Unity government, but she did not express her thoughts out loud. Her husband's outraged face as he heaped insults on all the military men in the world and on those in Chile in particular stopped her.

"It is true that the country has reached a point of polarization never before reached in its history," Elena thought.

"I myself have seen families divided, father against son, brother against brother, lifelong friends who now can't even say hello to each other.

"I have even seen my own house divided.

"It is true that the Popular Unity has brought us to the point of economic disaster. I have stood in line for four or five hours just to be able to buy the bare necessities in order to subsist.

"It is true that the country has not been working, for Julian himself admits that he has been spending most of his time at political meetings in his office.

"It is true that Chileans have been discriminated against according to their idealogy, for those who were not Marxists were considered fascists and found themselves being deprived of their jobs and prevented from any activity.

"It is true that to express oneself in the face of the threats and violence of an extremism that we had never known before was more and more difficult.

"It is true that they were trying to monopolize the education of our children to indoctrinate them with Marxist ideology right from their earliest years.

"It is true that it was pointless to report thieves and looters because the Marxist justice discriminated between 'good thieves'—the Marxists—and 'bad thieves'—the bourgeois.

"It is true that the president was nothing more than a puppet dancing between the fingers of the parties claiming to be loyal to the government.

"It is true that our farms were not producing, our industries were at a standstill, the offices were idle, the universities were at war, that the workers were living off the black market, that the professionals were leaving, that the extremists were arming themselves.

"No one can tell me that this is not true, for I have seen it with my own eyes and lived it myself, and nothing anyone can say will change my mind."

"They have been planning this for months, those hypocrites," said Julian, suddenly. "They were absolutely right, the marines who dared to denounce those planning the coup and were brutally tortured in Talcahuano. Altamirano was absolutely right to cry out for the creation of the People's Power.

"I didn't share his ideas and preferred Allende's peaceful methods, but now I am beginning to realize that if our people had been truly armed, the military would have thought twice before coming out of their barracks.

"Now they hold us defenseless. Nobody can stand up to them. All that we can do now is, as they say, to conform and obey.

"Our future will be to conform and obey forever and ever.

"And these soldiers have been trained like puppets, which is far worse. They have been trained like bears to dance, mesmerized by the tunes of the pipers of the Far Right.

"And the grand circus trainers are the Yankees!"

"Don't be a demagogue!" Elena protested. "You're behaving like a socialist candidate who has just lost an election."

"Oh, really? Do you really think the Yankees haven't been meddling in all this? Do you think the CIA wasn't encouraging all the strikes that were causing the shortages, and the long lines? Do you know how much each trucker was being paid who joined the strike? Even thousand escudos.

"Do you know how much that is in dollars? Three dollars!

"Can you imagine that ITT, Anaconda, Kennecott, and Ford were not willing to spend three dollars for each Chilean joining the strikers?"

"Quit your Castro histrionics, Julian! Neither you nor I know anything about how much money the Yankees coughed up for the strikes. But if you're talking about infiltrations, we all know that Chile has never before been so infiltrated by Cubans, Chinese, Tupamaros, Koreans, and all the rest of the 'Russian salad' which the Popular Unity wanted to feed us with. And if you don't want to open your eyes to this reality, you are turning your back on Chile."

"Me? Turning *my* back on Chile?" roared Julian, suddenly jumping to his feet. "And what about you, when *you* close your eyes to the Yankee grip that has been slowly strangling us till we vomit blood? You think I'm kidding? Isn't it Chilean blood that is being spilled right now? Do you believe that if the Yankees had let us breathe, this would be happening now? Who's the one who is turning his back on Chile, you or I?"

"I have never seen the Yankees sending our president crates marked 'art objects,' full of submachine guns.

"I have never seen them training guerrilla groups, nor parading in our streets haranguing against our institutions.

"I have never seen a North American president touring through our country lecturing us on how we should govern.

"I have never seen the streets and squares of Chile in the

163

towns and villages spattered with the names of North American politicians, peppered with the statues of North American politicians, and plastered with their photographs, with quotes from their pet phrases, with their flags, their hymns, their insignias, their slogans, their—"

"You're ridiculous! All that is just child's play, compared to the stranglehold of the Yankees. They don't come out into the streets because they don't care how we govern ourselves, just so long as we don't take away their power.

"They don't chant with our people, but they 'converse' in the offices and the living rooms of the rich.

"They don't send three or four crates full of submachine guns, but they buy our armies with their secondhand ships and tanks and planes.

· "Their presidents don't tour around our country because they are afraid of being spat on or killed by our people.

"They don't need to send 'advisers' to our president because it is our president who runs after them and trots off to Washington in order to be 'advised.'

"They don't need to train our guerrillas because our generals go to them to be trained. You'd have to be an idiot not to see these things."

"I forbid you to say in my presence that our armed forces are trotting after the Yankees! I'm willing to admit that the politicians in this country are only interested in making money, but I will not allow our soldiers' patriotism to be questioned.

"They are the only ones who have held themselves aloof from the sale of Chile to the highest bidder. And if they have intervened now, they have done so to pay off all the debts incurred by all the incompetent meddlers, all the mercenaries, all the traitors that have been manhandling Chile for far too long.

"They have run the risk of being called gorillas by imbeciles like you because they are willing to pay, not to sell. And to pay with their own money, sacrificing the only thing they have, which is their tradition of respect and loyalty for governments elected by the people. If you don't understand this sacrifice and cannot accept the difference that exists between our armed forces and the rest of the strongmen in the world, then it means that you have nothing left in you that is Chilean—not even the recollection of what your fatherland has been."

"I don't believe in this 'cash payment' you're speaking of. I believe that the only one who is paying is Allende!"

The morning of September 12 was a peaceful one for the Gonzaleses, or at least for Elena. She was able to buy food from a grocery located on the same block as her apartment building. She managed to do her marketing without violating the curfew, by entering the shop the back way, through the home of the shopkeeper, Don Flavio. She even managed to persuade him to sell her food she hadn't seen for months: tea, canned foods, ham—and even cigarettes for Julian!

What is more, the Italian shopkeeper, in an unprecedented gesture of generosity, presented her with two bars of chocolate for her children and opened a bottle of domestic champagne to celebrate with his customers what he called "the liberation of Chile."

There had been a general air of festivity in the little shop. All the women talked at the same time.

They were discussing the events of the day before, the eleventh, and the shootings during the night, as if it had all been part of a national holiday.

Most of them were "dropping names," of long-since forgotten relatives in the armed forces.

"My uncle, Colonel So-and-So, my godson, Adjutant to General What-not, I have a cousin Armored Car. No. 2 . . . "

Military terminology, completely foreign to them until that

moment, was bandied about. "Thirty caliber machine guns, Shermans, Hawker Hunters, rockets, recoilless rifles . . . "

A tone of admiration was used when referring to the efficiency of armored cars, the fantastic accuracy of the bombing, the discipline of the draftees, the propriety and courage of the officers.

A discovery had been made: Chile possessed armed forces that "worked" to perfection. At last, something was working in Chile! All their hopes depended on this discovery. The darkness of improvisation, pointless verbiage, squandering, inefficiency was over. The military, the new men, would build a new Chile.

Elena Gonzales felt an emotion long since dormant swell within her: patriotism.

To her surprise, she found herself remembering events, men, and women of the time of independence; she thought of her ambitions, her hopes, her sacrifices, and felt a warm and moving affinity with those names, places, and dates of history.

She felt reborn. Confused, Elena sensed a new strength arising within her, springing from the very fountainheads of the country, making her whole, urging her onward. To her surprise, she realized that, for the first time in her life, she was experiencing a desire to reread the forgotten history of her country.

"We are something that we ourselves have forgotten," she said to herself. "Now is the time to retrieve that forgotten identity."

She made plans to dig out old books, dust off the old, venerable names, and recharge her mind with their inspiration.

She would read these works to her sons, to Julian, she decided . . .

For a long time Elena had been groping her way through what to her seemed a nightmare of a Chile enveloped in mountains of paper painted with hate slogans, besieged by hundreds of thousands of feverishly aggressive faces, bristling with threatening fists, throbbing with parades, demonstrations, street fights, acts of sabotage, assaults; paralyzed by queues and strikes, a Chile at bitter war with itself and culminating in a president dying in a final "grand gesture" that will undoubtedly become one of the legends handed down to posterity, erasing from the Chileans' minds all remembrance of the dishonor of these last three years during which, in Elena's opinion, they had been deceived by a handful of thieves and incompetents.

"Heh, there," said Elena to her family as she entered her flat. "Guess what I've brought you."

She gave out the chocolate to the two boys and the cigarettes to Julian.

He lit one eagerly, but made no comment. He had noticed in his wife a merry and festive attitude which grieved and offended him. He preferred not to ask her any questions. He believed he knew what the answers would be and that they would only start them arguing again.

Julian did not have the stomach for another quarrel. He hadn't been able to sleep a wink all night.

He had felt as if every shot, every machine gun bullet were going through his own body, and he would writhe in his bed as if he were wounded, remaining awake through these nightmares, beside his serenely sleeping wife.

For Julian, Chile had just entered a dark age from which it would not emerge for God knows how many years. He felt as if he were at a funeral where even the lighted candles would soon be extinguished.

The dead body, symbolized by the riddled body of Allende, is the vast majority of the people: the poor. The gravediggers, those who are celebrating and toasting, are the usual minority: the rich, saved by the armed forces. The future is a night, a long sleepless night, tormented by the specters of hunger, injustice, persecution, and fear; a night that Julian is not sure he can accept, even to the point of seriously considering leaving the country or going underground.

In the space of just a few hours, his Chile had been snatched away. A Chile of the poor, a Chile that was laughing, singing, working, relaxing, living in a manner that apparently the wealthy could not accept. The pleasure of the poor is the displeasure of the rich. Life for the poor is death for the rich. And, once again, the rich are the winners and the poor the losers.

Julian felt a sadness he had never known before that day, because he had never realized how deeply he identified with "his" Chile.

"Would to God," he thought, "that I had never known the price would be defeat."

He had lost all hope the armed forces would champion the cause of the poor.

Their mandate for the coup had come from the rich, and the poor had had no say in the matter.

The rich mix only with the rich. The others, the peasants in the fields, the factory workers, the miners, the fishermen, are excluded from the dialogue, because they "don't know."

They don't know how to govern themselves; they only know how to follow orders. Obey and keep quiet if you want to achieve the only goal of your life: survival!

Julian's bitterness overwhelmed him. He could not even look at his wife. He lay down the book which he was pretending to read—it was impossible for him to continue, although the book was about Allende and was written by Debray—and he said, to nobody in particular, "Don't keep lunch for me."

Elena looked at him, plainly worried.

"But you can't go out in the street," she warned him.

"I'm going upstairs to Felipe's," Julian replied.

Elena stayed alone with the children. She preferred to let him do what he wanted. She could understand he did not want to stay cooped up, but she could not understand this need to Julian's to get away from her.

This senseless rift between them had been going on long enough. This too will have to change, she thought. And she was convinced that this change would come about, for in the new Chile whose rebirth she had witnessed today, families would not be broken up by politics. There would be no parties, just one country.

The children were eating. Elena pulled a chair up and opened the book she had in her hand.

"Listen," she said, and she began to read: "On September 18th, 1810. . . ."

"Don't talk such nonsense," said Dr. Felipe Torres to his friend, Julian. "No one can suppress the Left. Nobody can suppress the South, for example, and leave just the North. There will always be the South, there will always be the Left. I assure you that even among the members of the junta, there have to be some who are left of the others."

"That's sophistry," Julian interrupted him impatiently. "It is incredible that you cannot accept a fact of life. Chile has no left wing now, like a bird whose wing has been clipped off to stop it from flying. Listen, I want to be quite frank, I came here to get drunk, not to argue. I don't have the strength to argue, so get out your bottles of booze or I'll leave."

Felipe smiled, got out a bottle of brandy and two glasses, and filled them. Julian emptied his glass in one gulp and went for a refill. Felipe watched him in silence.

At last, he said, "Julian you must understand, it is your Left that has been defeated, not *the* Left. And your Left defeated itself, through inefficiency."

Julian shook his head vigorously.

"You don't understand a thing," he said. "All you are doing are theorizing and completely disregarding the tragedy we are going through. The poor, you understand?, it is the poor who have been defeated!"

"The poor do not belong exclusively either to the Left or the Right, although each of the two sides would like to claim them as exclusive property," remarked Felipe, looking at his friend with concern. "I'm very much afraid that they have been filling your head with trash."

Julian gulped down another brandy by way of an answer. His friend's company was now beginning to pall. No one seemed to understand that this was not the time for discussion.

But neither could Felipe Torres keep his feelings bottled up. He was not only edgy, but angry. He looked at Julian and felt his anger swell inside him.

"Stop feeling like a victim! I don't care if you do look at me like that. What you have to understand once and for all is that you were the *villain*, not the victim.

"You were the accomplice of a left wing that was a monumental failure, not only on a national scale but also on a continental and world scale. And don't come out now with that old refrain of the North American imperialism and fascist conspiracy which was just not true of yesterday *or* today.

"If, instead of governing for the twenties, Allende and his friends had governed for the seventies, there would have been no imperialism or fascism to speak of.

"Your coalition was antiquated, insolvent, frivolous, improvident, completely unprepared scientifically and technically, convinced that it could keep the country happy simply with speeches, demonstrations, and paper money.

"Chile was too big for the Popular Unity to handle. You left-wingers proved that all the Left is good for is vociferating from the opposition benches, but when it governs, it just shits.

"Wait a minute, I know that you don't want to listen anymore. You don't want to listen, because it hurts. But you're not the only one who is hurt, you know. It hurts me too, to see what has happened to this country, because it doesn't deserve it.

"I never had much to do with the Popular Unity government, even if I did vote for it, but let me tell you this, I would be ashamed to go around moaning that the CIA pulled my pants down and gave me a good thrashing.

"I would be ashamed to run around the world begging for compassion from other countries. The true shame, the only shame you have to face up to is that your defeat was brought about by your own inadequacies. And you have only yourselves to blame for that. If you don't learn these lessons, the Left can never be the government in Chile again."

Julian Gonzales was no longer listening. This conversation had become too painful.

At last, he said, "And you think that all these flames, this smoke, these deaths that we see now are frivolity?"

Felipe would not be distracted.

"If this had been a mature left wing," he replied, "and if the majority of the country had been satisfied with it, these flames, this smoke, these deaths which we are seeing now would have been multiplied a hundred thousand times, because of the fiery resistance put up against a coup.

"You can rest assured, this was a poor funeral for a poor government, which was only great in the dreams of Allende, the First Dreamer of the Republic.

"Don't you think we've had enough dreams of making history at our country's expense and at the expense of its very existence? It was very nice to make the headlines in all the biggest newspapers throughout the world as an 'interesting experiment.'

"But who is paying for that experiment? France, Germany, Italy? What do you think *they'll* do now? They'll shed a few tears of mourning and turn their eyes to more interesting places.

"What was the point of all this? How long did it last? How much did it cost us? What do you want? To go on dreaming? You have to wake up, Julian!

"For a lot of people, waking up will be very painful. Some will wake up in exile, others in prison, others in misery, and others will die before they wake up. But for God's sake, let's have done with these dreams!

"We are a poor country, remote, ignored, alone, but this is a real place, where the real new Left must arise, with leaders unshackled by historic dreams and alert to what we truly are and have, with the best professionals and experts available in the country, capable of putting it back on its feet and showing to whoever is watching that the Left is more efficient and beneficial for all Chileans, here and now.

"With students prepared to head their faculties not on the basis of their propaganda slogans, but on the basis of their qualifications, the workers and the farm laborers will be able to *see,* not just *hear* that the Left is worthy of their blood to defend it.

"Then the armed forces would have something more to defend than a mere collection of constitutional pacts. Then the Right would need something more than North American support to defend its positions.

"It is for the sake of this alert, modern Chilean Left that I cannot afford the cowardly luxury of considering myself beaten."

Julian Gonzales gazed into his empty glass. He was confused. He could not resign himself to classifying so many decades of progressive struggle, such a courageous and altruistic leader as a mere Chilean Dream or Dreamer.

He was aware that the country was bankrupt. His work at the bank had allowed him access to some of the figures.

The deficit for the fiscal year of 1972 had reached 40 percent of the total expenditure and had been financed with new bill issues. The tax revenue in foreign currency had decreased by 54 percent from the previous year. The estimated rate of inflation for 1973 was 388 percent, a world record. The prices for consumer products were rising at a pace of 287 percent per annum. Nationalized enterprises were showing losses that would have to be absorbed by new currency issues, with the result that the amount of money in circulation was increasing at the rate of 300 percent per annum. Food imports had increased by 54 percent. The foreign debt was increasing at the rate of $1,200,000 per day. Industrial production for the year 1973 would be 6 percent lower than that of the previous year. Agricultural production was down 22 percent. Copper production was expected to decrease by 5 percent during 1973. Iron production had decreased by 31 percent, niter was down 13 percent, coal was down 12 percent, petroleum 3 percent. The acreage under construction in 1972 had reached only 48 percent of that developed in 1971.

Failure by the government, or "triumph" by the opposition? Villain or victim? Julian Gonzales could not decide. His friend had done so already: the government was guilty, and the Left had to be rebuilt.

Felipe filled the glasses again while waiting for a reply from Julian, but in that moment, the tiny attic was shaken by the whirring of a military helicopter flying a few yards above the building.

Julian's nerves had been sorely tried during the last thirty hours of forced seclusion. He rushed to the balcony and shouted at the helicopter now fading away in the distance, "You sons of bitches, you sons of bitches."

Felipe ran up behind him and tried to calm him down,

but Julian seemed to have completely lost control of himself.

"Shut up, you idiot!" Felipe said, shoving him back inside the room. "The place is crawling with soldiers! Don't you think there have been enough 'suicides'?"

Julian slumped into the armchair. He was pale, and sweat stood out on his brow. He could not tell whether it was the brandy that had gone to his head, or whether it was his whole being that was rebelling against the pressure he had lived through during the last two days. But already he felt calmer.

Felipe brought him a glass of water and instructed him to swallow a few pills.

"You must calm down and put all of this out of your mind for several hours," he said.

Julian shook his head.

"I cannot forget," he said. "You can, but I cannot. I am with the Left that died fighting. I am with Allende, with the one single truly revolutionary moment in the life of Allende—his death. I feel it in my guts. I cannot agree with you. And please forgive me for this exhibition of hysterics I've subjected you to. It's just that I feel so tired and so—so exhausted."

Julian made a gesture to get up from the chair and go away, but Felipe held him back with a gesture.

"Wait," he said. "There remains so much to be said, so much to think about. All I want you to remember for now is that a left wing that imposes itself by force of arms can only last by force of arms. And the Left that I am dreaming of must command attention and respect in order to be effective."

From the door, Julian looked at his friend and laughed gently.

"It seems to me that the First Dreamer of the Republic was you, and not Allende," he said.

"Time will tell," Felipe replied.

"Time—" repeated Julian Gonzales to himself in the elevator

which took him back to his floor. "How much time? Ten years, twenty, thirty—?"

But one piece of friendly advice he would follow: to get some sleep.

And Julian Gonzales slept all that afternoon, not awaking until the sun was setting. He got up, took a shower, and, feeling hungry, went into the kitchen.

Scarcely believing his eyes, he saw Elena at that moment, hanging out a flag on the apartment terrace, the sign of allegiance to the junta. With a shout, Julian rushed forward to stop her.

The sun was sinking behind the hills of the coastal Cordilleras, and the Andes acquired a rosy blush in sympathy. Between the two mountain ranges, Santiago began to light up for the night. At nightfall the armed forces' patrols double their vigilance, for it is the hour of the sniper.

A jeep carrying five soldiers under the command of an officer was patrolling a middle-class residential quarter, deserted on account of the curfew. All seemed calm. Suddenly, the officer raised his arm and the jeep stopped.

"Is something wrong, captain?"

The sergeant clutched his gun and, glancing up and down the street, tried to spot what had caught the attention of his superior.

The officer made a reassuring gesture, climbed down from the jeep, and casually walked over to where he had seen the national flag fall.

He picked it up, folded it carefully, and placed it in one of his jacket pockets. He then looked up at the fourth floor of the large apartment building and said to the man and woman who were watching him from the terrace, "Is this flag yours?"

"Yes!" they replied in unison, but somewhat uneasily. "We dropped it by mistake."

THE GONZALESES

Julian and Elena Gonzales continued to stare nervously at the soldier whose face had assumed a doubting expression. At last, the officer turned around and slowly walked back to his jeep.

"Hey!" cried Julian. "That's our flag!"

The officer stopped, looked up, and replied in a jovial tone, "We'll return it to you when you know how to take proper care of it!"

In silence, Elena and Julian Gonzales watched the jeep as it disappeared down the quiet streets of Santiago.

EPILOGUE

June 6, 1974

Laura Allende continues to live in Chile. In the days immediately following the coup she was under house arrest, but it was not enforced. Instead, she continued to receive her regular medical treatment and was able to use the excuse of seeing the doctor to keep track of her friends.

One of her four children, Pedro Gaston, sought asylum in the Ecuadorian embassy during the coup. He now lives in Mexico with his wife and children. Her other two children remain in Chile.

Her daughter Denise is also in Mexico. Her other daughter Marian lives with Laura. Andres is head of the Movement of the Revolutionary Left and is underground.

"Andres chose his road, and I can do nothing to stop him," explains Laura.

Hortensia Bussi de Allende   Together with her daughters, Beatriz and Isabel, she has left Chile, for Mexico and Cuba, where she is active in opposing the junta.

Miriam Contreras Bell (La Payita)   After her escape from the Moneda on the eleventh, she took refuge in the Swedish embassy, where she stayed until receiving safe-conduct to travel to Sweden in June.

Eduardo Novoa   This key figure in the Allende government today lives in Mexico, where he is a professor of penal law at the University of Mexico.

Carlos Briones   A minister of the interior under Allende, today he works in Chile as a lawyer, specializing in social security and workers' rights. He shares an office with his wife, also a lawyer, who worked for the Justice Department in the Popular Unity government.

After the coup Briones was put under house arrest, but he was soon allowed freedom of movement and took up his former position as professor of law at the University of Chile Law School. He recently resigned from the faculty, declaring that a university controlled by the military is at variance with the concept of a free institution committed to social change.

Every other minister in Allende's government was detained on Dawson Island. When asked why he was not involved in the trials of many of his former colleagues, held in Santiago in the spring of 1974, Briones replied, "I would have liked to defend my comrades who are awaiting trial, but I have not done so because I fear that as a lawyer associated with leftish ideas I will always be viewed with mistrust."

José Toha   Toha, a personal friend of Salvador Allende, a journalist and writer, was active in many ministries in the popular Unity government. He was detained on Dawson Island, where he subsequently fell sick, and died in the Military Hospital of Santiago in April 1974.

Cardinal Raul Silva Henriquez   The head of the Chilean Catholic Church, Cardinal Henriquez has been very active inside Chile, both in trying to unite all Chileans and in protecting those who have lost power. He is one of the few voices in Chile calling for harmony and sanity which the junta allows to be heard. Together with other church leaders, he organized the Committee of Cooperation for Peace in Chile, which is particularly concerned with the welfare of those under arrest.

Carlos Jorquera   Jorquera was detained at Dawson Island and is now awaiting his trial in Santiago.

Admiral Patricio Carvajal   He is now minister of Foreign Affairs.

General Javier Palacios   Palacios, who led the final assault on the Moneda, is now in charge of the Department for the Development of Production (CORFO).

Eduardo Frei   He is in the United States, where he will give a course at a New York University. Afterward he intends to go to Europe.

Patricio Aylwin   President of the Christian Democratic Party, he continues to live in Santiago, where he is writing a book about Chilean law.

Bernardo Leighton   One of the founders of the Christian Democratic Party, he decided to live in Rome in voluntary exile. The junta has since prohibited his return to Chile, owing to declarations he has made against the regime.

Jorge Alessandri   A recluse, very little is known of his life since he lost the 1970 presidential election to Allende and the Popular Unity coalition. He is president of the Paper and Manufacturing Company, based in Santiago.

Pablo Rodriguez   Founder of the "Fatherland and Liberty" nationalist movement in 1970 in opposition to the election of Allende, today he lives in Chile, works as a lawyer, collaborates with the junta in an unofficial capacity, and writes a column on contemporary topics for the Santiago daily newspapers *La Ter-cera* and *La Segunda.*

Leon Vilarin President of the National Confederation of Truck Owners, whose strike in the fall of 1973 was instrumental in the fall of the Allende government, today he travels regularly to other countries to defend the junta.

"Chile is recuperating . . . a true democracy exists . . . the government has committed errors, but it has the courage and integrity to recognize them, and what is better, to remedy them."

In February 1973, for the first time in 150 years, the flowering *quilla* suddenly dried up all over the country. According to an old Mapuche Indian legend, it is a portent of sorrow and great changes.

Right up to the coup in September 1973, the Mapuche performed religious ceremonies which called on their gods to protect them from what was to come. The gods did not listen.

In June 1974, the *quilla* is beginning to revive.

Florencia Varas